M000033737

MARKET FORCES

STRATEGIC TRENDS IMPACTING SENIOR LIVING PROVIDERS

JILL J. JOHNSON, MBA

Other books by Jill J. Johnson:

From the BOLD Questions Series:

BOLD Questions – Business Strategy Edition

BOLD Questions – Opportunities Edition

BOLD Questions – Leadership Edition

BOLD Questions – Decision Making Edition

Compounding Your Confidence:
Strategies to Expand Your Opportunities for Success

Enduring Enterprises (coming soon)

Learn more about Jill online and check out
her free white papers at
www.jcs-usa.com

MARKET FORCES

STRATEGIC TRENDS IMPACTING SENIOR LIVING PROVIDERS

JILL J. JOHNSON, MBA

Market Forces: Strategic Trends Impacting Senior Living Providers

Copyright © 2019 Jill J. Johnson

Published by Johnson Consulting Services
Minneapolis, Minnesota
www.jcs-usa.com

All rights reserved.
No part of this publication may be reproduced, stored in a retrieval system, or transmitted in any form or by any means, electronic, mechanical, photocopying, recording, scanning, or otherwise, without written permission from the author.

Limit of liability/disclaimer of warranty:
While the publisher and author have used their best efforts in preparing this book, they make no representations or warranties with respect to the accuracy or completeness of the contents of this book and specifically disclaim any implied warranties of merchantability or fitness for a particular purpose. The advice and strategies contained herein may not be suitable for your situation. This work is sold on the understanding that the publisher and author are not engaged in rendering professional services. Neither the publisher or author shall be liable for damages arising herefrom. If professional advice or other expert assistance is required, the services of a competent professional should be sought.

Book Edited by Jan McDaniel

Book Design by Chris Mendoza, CAMM. arts LLC. www.chrisdmendoza.com

For information on Jill or on how to order bulk copies of this book, contact her at: www.jcs-usa.com

ISBN 978-0-9984236-5-4

1. Business   2. Non-Fiction   3. Real Estate

Printed in the United States of America

Author's Note

This is a work of creative nonfiction. The situations and events are portrayed to the best of my memory. While all the stories and case studies in this book are true, names and identifying details have been changed to protect the privacy of the people and clients involved. The conversations and observations described in the book all come from my recollections and from my research.

This book is dedicated to my clients who provide services to seniors

You have accepted one of the most demanding professional challenges possible – to walk with older adults as they navigate the transitions of aging. Your compassion and caring have been an inspiration to me. You challenge me to bring the best of my abilities to provide you with the insight you need to ensure our industry continues to make a difference in the future to older adults and their families. I have learned so much from all of you about what the word "service" truly means.

MARKET FORCES:
Strategic Trends Impacting
Senior Living Providers

Contents

Introduction 1

Chapter 1 – The Strategic Impact of Market Forces 7

Chapter 2 – Operating in a VUCA World.................................13

Chapter 3 – The Strategic Impact of Evolving Demographics 23

Chapter 4 – The Birth Dearth 31

Chapter 5 – The Strategic Impact of Demographics on Pricing 37

Chapter 6 – The Strategic Impact of Competition 51

Chapter 7 – Curb Appeal...65

Chapter 8 – The Strategic Impact of Health Care 73

Chapter 9 – The Strategic Impact of Other Market Forces 85

Chapter 10 – The Strategic Impact of Programming.............97

Chapter 11 – The Need for Deeper Strategic Thinking 111

Chapter 12 – Final Thoughts...119

About Jill Johnson...125

Acknowledgments 127

Introduction

The volatile economy we have been experiencing has buffeted just about every industry. Senior living organizations have not been immune to these economic and market trend challenges. The senior living providers who survive and even thrive in this complex environment are those who do not accept the status quo. Nor do they just hope their economic or marketplace situations will magically keep their communities full.

The senior living industry encompasses one of the most complex business operations you will ever encounter. It comprises the elements of many different types of enterprises. At its core, it means multi-family housing targeted to a specific age segment. Yet senior living providers often are involved in the delivery of both simple and complex healthcare. You also handle hospitality, dining services, social services, entertainment, transportation, spiritual care, facility management, landscaping, fitness center services, salon and spa services, and even convenience store operations. Plus, it is all wrapped up in the complexities of providing service and care for aging adults who are moving toward or through their final transitions of life. Even those of you focusing on active adult housing or age-restricted housing with no services will eventually be faced with residents who have aged in place but can no longer live in their home without assistance.

It is common knowledge that there is a "Senior Tsunami" in population emerging which will create many ongoing pressures for the industry and the need for our services. Some providers will thrive as they are able to expand to meet the needs of underserved segments in their communities.

But it is not so simple. There are many deeper market forces at play beyond demographic totals that may have serious repercussions influencing the demand for senior housing and its services. These market forces have the potential to shift demand as the seismic disruption of aging becomes more apparent. The undercurrents of these market forces are often missed as discussions generally focus only on the bigger demographic trends but do not consider the depth of the unnoticed waves of the other shifts bubbling underneath them.

Senior living leaders, their boards and staff - and those considering entering this industry for the first time - all need to better understand the market forces impacting senior services. This is vital as many of those forces are beyond your control. You need to understand and better anticipate the impact of these market forces so you can figure out how you will survive and thrive no matter what happens.

It doesn't matter whether you are a freestanding nursing home facility, offer a full continuum of care or whether your focus is active adult, independent and/or assisted living. There might be differences in your operational issues or market perspectives, but there are many hard questions you should consider and act on which apply broadly throughout the senior living sector.

Recently I spoke at an industry conference where the theme was, "Be Your Difference." This theme resonated deeply with me. As my team and I work with senior living providers around the United States and review the markets they are operating in, we see just how much confusion is emerging. Calls we get from those serving seniors in other countries show confusion too.

Consumers are being inundated with so many different promotional messages it is becoming exceptionally difficult for them to fully understand what is actually being offered by providers and what are the real costs. Frankly, the consumers' confusion arises because we are not always clear about what we are offering. Providers are trying to be everything to everybody to adjust for the reality of the soft occupancy many of you are experiencing but are reluctant to talk about.

Some providers are doing exceptionally well in this environment. But this is not the universal experience. Concerns abound across the country among executives leading wonderful senior living communities who are struggling to understand, along with their boards of directors and leadership teams, why their sites are not fully occupied. They feel embarrassed and frustrated because they are being told the "Senior Tsunami" should be generating massive demand, yet their own sites are not full. They are struggling with the pressure to understand who or what they should blame and how to tackle the dilemma.

This book will provide you with a deeper perspective on what is typically driving much of these occupancy issues. The insight passed along here will help those of you having occupancy and other challenges to better understand what is really going on within this demographic "Tsunami" and how the other market forces impacting this industry are challenging you today and may impact your long-term future.

Some of the occupancy challenge is clearly due to the significant competitive expansion and development activity that has emerged in recent years. But there is more to it than this. As a longtime consultant to senior living providers who are operating in highly competitive markets or who are in trouble, I am going to pull back the curtain to candidly share with you what we really see happening in these marketplaces. I will share with you why providers are struggling to cope and fill their properties -- and the underlying reasons for why this is happening to them. This may help bring clarity to what is happening to you as well.

Over the course of the last three decades of working in the senior living industry, I have personally visited more than 2,000 senior living communities across the nation. I have studied at least a thousand more.

I have had the opportunity to talk with providers in other countries as well. What works in one nation, state, county or town will not necessarily work in another market. Small towns and rural providers have different challenges than providers operating in major cities. Providers on the east coast have different consumer dynamics in their markets than providers based on the west coast or in the north or south. Providers in other countries are developing their own approaches to meet the needs of their aging population.

Each market has its own uniqueness based on the people who live there, the depth of their acceptance of senior housing, and what consumers have come to expect. As a result, getting solid market insight and accurate market intelligence on the local community you serve is fundamental to developing successful strategies designed to stabilize your occupancy or help you design your plans for the future. Cookie cutter approaches are not enough to guarantee success.

To be successful in the senior living industry requires a bold set of clear and strong strategies based on a careful study of your market. Most providers only do this in a cursory manner. I'm not talking about just doing a quick scan of the landscape or getting a few competitor anecdotes and then making some simple assumptions. The real answers are found by using a more sophisticated research approach and asking better questions that get to the root causes of your challenges and gaining better insights that you can leverage for success.

To be successful in the evolving senior living industry, it also takes more than just the ability to coordinate your team's activities for service delivery. Ultimately, your leadership effectiveness will require an even deeper level of critical thinking as you engage in your decision-making. There are many serious questions facing senior living leadership and your boards, but if you look at it from the perspective of your potential customer base, you and your enterprise will be much better served.

Some of you may be faced with tough decisions. This will be especially true for those of you who are existing providers operating in increasingly competitive marketplaces. Is it time for you to look at renovating your physical plant? Do you need to adjust some of your service lines? Do you need to review and adjust your mix of employees or their salary structure to be more customer-focused? Do you need to rethink your pricing?

In this book, I am going to share some deep insights about three key factors to help guide your thinking and strategies toward creating sustainable enterprises. First, consider what are the market forces going on around you today. I am going to spend the most time discussing market forces because they are the primary drivers of what is impacting the senior living industry now and into the future. The second component will review the implications of these market forces for you as you begin to study your campuses and developments with a more detached assessment. Finally, I will provide you with strategic insights based on what I have observed in operational and physical plant trends in various parts of the country as providers have begun to adapt to these market forces that you can consider for your own senior living communities.

While this is not intended to cover every possible situation, this book is intended to stimulate your thinking and help you prepare more strategically for the complex future ahead. The stories and insight shared here focus on the U.S. market, but the implications are comparable in other countries as well.

A colleague of mine is fond of saying, "Never waste a crisis." What she means is a crisis is an opportunity to learn, grow, and thrive if we take hard looks at the underlying causes and act to correct them. Outside consulting experts like me are usually called in to work with senior living communities when they are in crisis. Nearly all of them got into trouble because they missed or ignored one or more of the key insights I am going to share with you in this book. The savviest providers are those who make the time to better understand the shifting market forces before they cause a catastrophe to their occupancies, licensing, reimbursements, staffing, resident satisfaction or financial health. We can all agree the sooner you acknowledge and get ahead of your pain, the more quickly you can sustain or recover a healthy market position. Considering the ramifications of the evolving market forces will prepare you to weather any storm.

Chapter 1
The Strategic Impact
of Market Forces

There are multiple market forces impacting the success of organizations such as yours or the one you may be considering for development. Understanding these market forces is essential to understanding the pressures impacting every aspect of your organization and your strategy development. These key market forces are the underlying trends which are driving your potential for success, your occupancy, and may be driving the need for your senior living community to change. Making those critical adjustments will determine if your enterprise endures.

Over the years, I have identified **nine market forces** that significantly impact the senior living industry. Here is the list to help you get started thinking about how market forces impact your senior living community or your development potential. We'll go into each of these in greater detail later in this book.

- **Demographics:** Demographics are the objective characteristics of your target market that you can measure. Demographics are more than a total population number. They also include specific character-istics about your consumers such as age, gender, household size, income level or ethnicity. These characteristics are typically review-ed in combination in senior living market studies. For example, you might combine an age range with household income for a specific geographic area. You may find you have a different demographic make-up for each of your sites if you operate a multi-site enterprise. Perhaps the target market you have grown used to serving might have aged-out of needing you. Or there may be too few of them to recruit to your campus because the costs associated with living at your site are much higher than they can actually afford. Demographics are fundamental to being able to accurately count your prospective consumers, help you determine if you are still feasible in your market area, and to identify if there are emerging opportunities.

• **Generational Differences:** Think about the people you employ. You have multiple generations trying to work together. You have people who have different educational experiences, different attitudes about how they want to work, as well as different attitudes about pay and benefits. Your customers are changing too in what they factor into their purchasing decisions or what they value in a senior living environment. This holds true for the adult children of your prospective residents. Each generation has a slightly different approach to problem-solving. They also have different attitudes about money in terms of saving for their long-term needs, their willingness to spend their money, and their attitude towards taking on debt. Adult children have different views about spending their parent's money. Their attitudes impact their willingness to pay the bills for the care their parents receive from you or their willingness to support the choice their parents make to move into your community.

• **Competitors:** As new competitors enter your market they often change your consumers' expectations about pricing, services, and amenities. They may even redefine how you are perceived. Are your competitors changing the way your residents' needs are satisfied? Are they bringing enhanced amenities or new technology into your market? Are their salary and benefit structures more in tune with your local employment market than you? Each of these competitive factors will require a reassessment to make sure you can continue to compete when your competition is changing your staff and consumers' expectations.

- **Economic Impacts:** Clearly the shifts and changes in the economy drive what happens to you. Your operating costs may go up. When using history as a guide, it is only a matter of time before another recession will hit. It is not **_if_** economic forces will change; it is **_when_** and **_how deeply_** disruptive they will be. In most industries, a recession impacts consumers' willingness to spend money on items that are considered non-essential. Business clients respond by retrenching from buying outside services or by laying off employees. They stop unnecessary business travel. Vendors begin applying harsher credit terms to ensure they get paid. In the senior living industry, retirees postpone their moves and look for lower cost alternatives to support them at home. They wait until they absolutely need more help and they sometimes wait too long.

- **Operating Costs:** It is expensive to do business today. Each type of business has different variables impacting their operating costs. Senior living is no exception. In a perfect world, you would be able to directly pass along all of the increased costs to your residents. But sometimes those operating costs are increasing at a faster rate than the rate increases your residents can afford or are willing to pay. You have to calibrate your prices to your market. You have to very carefully consider what services you include in your prices not only to account for the shifting winds of the economy, but also to reflect the impact rate increases will have on who can afford your site.

- **Governmental Influences:** Government intervention in your operation can hit at the local, regional, state or federal level. Changes in employment requirements and government mandates impact your profitability. Regulatory constraints and the costs of compliance are constantly influencing your senior living community. For those of you serving higher care residents, you likely now face daily challenges due to reduced health care reimbursement and the impact of expanded regulations. It is clearly daunting at best. The constant shifts in reimbursement and increased use of Medicare Advantage plans adds to the growing instability of providing care at a rate that covers your costs.

• **Capital Markets:** As interest rates rise, access to capital may fall. If you need to borrow money to renovate or expand your physical plant, the cost of capital will have an impact on you. It impacts how much you can borrow and how much it will cost you to pay it back. That too will impact your pricing and what your market can afford. As access to credit changes, this may shift the need for services such as yours. The ability to borrow money may be impacting your potential residents too. If people cannot borrow, maybe your future residents cannot sell their homes to be able to move into your campus.

• **Technology:** The development and deployment of technology is a game changer in many industries. Personal computers have more power than the large mainframe systems from the early era of computing. Robotics and manufacturing technologies are reducing the need for employees in certain industry sectors. The advent of the Internet has changed how consumers shop and how buyers seek information. As consumers are becoming more comfortable shopping online, it is altering the need for brick and mortar stores. In some industries, technology is now replacing people in the workforce. In senior living communities, access to the Internet has changed how consumers evaluate your sites and determine if you are the right fit for their lifestyle or their parents. Emerging technologies may alter how the chronic diseases of older adults are monitored and managed. Other technological trends may offer new options for offsetting staffing shortages or enhancing your team's productivity in ways that have not been considered. As a leader, you have to evaluate the cost of implementing new technologies relative to the cost savings they could eventually generate. You also have to be mindful of whether your employees and residents are both willing and able to adapt to innovation.

• **Industry Changes:** Every industry has its optimal methods for doing business called Best Practices. Industries that deal with perishables have tips and tricks to keep those items fresher longer. Other industries have identified high-quality approaches for dealing with employees or incorporating technology. Industries evolve based on new innovations and emerging options to address challenges. The senior living industry is not immune to these changes either. Staying abreast of what is new in this industry is vital to identifying emerging options to enhance your customer service. Evolving Best Practices in each aspect of your complex enterprise offer new options for considering strategic adjustments in cost savings, marketing, staff recruitment, and every area of your operation.

When you consider how these nine key market forces impact your strategies, think about how you can access the information you will need to more fully understand how each of these market forces could impact your senior living enterprise. Then consider how you can leverage this information to identify the most critical evolving trends. If you do this, you will be better able to focus your time and your talent on addressing the most essential changes you will need to implement to make sure your enterprise survives.

Chapter 2
Operating in a VUCA World

The world in which you now operate is what those of us who are involved in strategy work call VUCA. VUCA stands for Volatile, Uncertain, Complex and Ambiguous. We live in a world where there is increasing complexity within the consumer base we serve, their families, and the competitive markets in which we operate.

There are two other things driving change in senior living, as well as in many other industries. As they impact market forces, there is little you can do to influence them. Rather, you must consider how you are going to adapt to them. The more ahead of the curve you are, the better able you will be to pilot test or consider your options and refine your strategic response long before a crisis emerges.

The first driver is referred to as **pre-determined events**. These events are inevitable. They are the circumstances we know (or could know with a little effort). On an individual level, we know that all of our residents will die and many are likely to get sicker on our watch. For some of you, the programs, services, people, and resources you offer to residents will delay the inevitable and improve their quality of life. This is the powerful impact of the work you and your teams do every day. Yet it will not prevent your need for continually having to replace your customer base to maintain your occupancy.

One of the most significant pre-determined events impacting senior living today is the impact of demographic shifts. You can buy demographic data for nearly every market and break it down into exceptionally discrete segments to review your opportunities and risk. My management consulting firm constantly buys this type of data to evaluate what demographic shifts and trends in the local market will impact our clients and their customers. We also conduct an even deeper dive of the demographic data to look for micro-impacts that go beyond only considering generic across the board trends.

We carefully study the detailed breakdown of different age cohorts, income disparities and/or chronic health conditions. There are many different issues impacting subsets within this broad age cohort of older adults and these issues will impact your customers in significantly different ways. You need to consider what are the pre-determined events likely to impact your senior living community. Once you have the right data and information identified, you can consider the long-term impact of this information and anticipate critical challenges you will likely face.

The second driver of change is referred to as the **critical uncertainties**. These are the issues that are unpredictable while still remaining a matter of choice in how you deal with them or in how they will evolve within your marketplace. These critical uncertainties could include changes in government regulations or new competitor challenges such as price cuts, the opening of new competitive developments, the expansion of new service offerings or advanced technology. This could include shifts and changes in how seniors save or spend which may impact whether, or if, they can pay for your services and offerings. These are the change drivers you need to identify and anticipate so you can consider how to respond. When the consideration of critical market forces such as demographics are utilized in a serious and professional manner, you have a powerful opportunity to consider a variety of strategic considerations and risks.

Successful senior living communities stay on top of the drivers of change and the evolving market forces to anticipate how their business strategies may have to adapt in the future. Unfortunately, this can be tough in an industry like ours. Those enterprises that have been successful over the years have not only been alert to the coming changes; they also proactively implement clever ways for adapting to changes and responding with thoughtfulness before the changes impact revenues rather than merely responding reactively. They have developed innovations and piloted them to work the kinks out before investing significant resources to deploy them more broadly. Doing the deeper dive allows you and your board to better anticipate critical market shifts and stay on top of how to navigate them through turbulent times.

Even if you operate a relatively small site or are located in a rural area, you still have the capacity to use the resources of local associations and governmental data sources. You can usually access databases at your local library to research and study these trends, expected shifts and the options available to implement change. You can also purchase demographic data relatively inexpensively to provide you the insight you need.

Ever since David slew Goliath in the Bible, it is clear that success is often more a matter of the effectiveness of the strategies that have been deployed rather than the size or scale of the enterprise. This is how enduring senior living communities approach their long-term view. Thinking about your customers and deeply considering the opportunities you have available to serve them frees you to focus most of your efforts on what is going to drive your residents' satisfaction. Their satisfaction will ultimately drive your occupancy and revenue.

When you look back at the era during the Great Recession that started in 2008, do you remember how hard that period was? It was an exceptionally tough economic environment in which to strategically navigate. We kept our eyes on the Federal Reserve, among other things, to help us gauge interest rates. We all watched closely to determine whether, how and/or if the investment markets would ever stabilize.

Most providers understood that the unstable economy was wreaking havoc on their customers. Older adults were reeling from the significant drop in their net worth and home value. They were desperately uncertain about their ability to have enough savings for the remainder of their lives. Clearly, these factors impacted our future residents' ability to pay for their Golden Years.

Many investment professionals have privately shared with me in the intervening years that a number of older adults panicked during this Great Recession period. They were deeply afraid they would lose everything, so they took what they viewed as the safer bet and cashed out their investments. But when they did this, they locked in their investment losses. These were not paper losses. These decisions resulted in real reductions in their net worth.

Frankly, few senior living leaders or their boards are candidly discussing how they will thrive in the future if their prospective residents can no longer afford the entrance fees or high monthly costs for their sites. Our clients do talk about these issues and it shapes how they are responding to their pricing strategies, their community education, and their conversations with prospects.

During the era of the Great Recession, younger seniors responded by putting off an early retirement or went back to work. If they did move, they went to a "carefree living" or "maintenance free" living environment rather than selecting a senior living community offering housing with services. They were unsure if they could even sell their home to finance their move to a senior living community, much less get enough money out of their home sale to meet any entrance fee requirement.

Some of these older adults are the future customers our industry hopes to serve over the next decade. When they locked in their investment losses, some of them experienced a drop of as much as 30 to 50 percent of their net worth. The sad truth is these older adults will never recover the monies they lost. As a result, their options for the retirement housing they had expected would be in their distant future have disappeared because it is no longer affordable to them. This financial shift is now requiring them to quietly begin considering a Plan B or Plan C. Or worse, they are using the monies of their parents, who the industry is serving now, and reducing the cash and liquidity their parents have available to pay your fees.

The critical uncertainty the Great Recession has created is a question regarding whether seniors we have expected will be our customers realistically can be ours in the future. Over the next decade and beyond, the issue of affordability is likely to take on an even greater importance than ever before. It is a key area that many providers should consider as they ponder how to help prospective residents deal with or develop their Plan B or C.

One other critical uncertainty to consider are anomalies called **Black Swan** events. Black Swan events are often described as circumstances we cannot anticipate or control. Many people have described the market collapse of the Great Recession as being a Black Swan event. I always push back on this comment and say, "How could you really call this a Black Swan? We were due for another major market correction and recession."

Now of course, like everyone else, I certainly did not anticipate the last recession would be as deep or as painful as it was, but it was inevitable that some level of significant economic constriction would occur within that approximate window of time. And it will again. We can count on the fact there will be another economic correction. Unfortunately, you just never can predict with certainty when it will occur, how deep it will be or how long it will last.

Black Swan events are uncontrollable and can be catastrophic. They can have earth-shattering consequences for just about every organization. This could be the terrible events that occurred on September 11, 2001 or the breaking of a dam due to the aftermath of a hurricane.

I bet some of you were the only game in town when you originally opened years ago. But today you have major new competition. Competition creates a totally different dynamic for a senior living enterprise because when you have to really compete for residents, you will be competing with other providers who are newer, prettier, and often using more sophisticated (and effective) marketing than you ever needed when you were the only available option. The advent of all this new competition may feel like a Black Swan to you, even though you knew it was coming.

This expanded competitive pressure is likely to be challenging for your teams. In many cases, they have grown accustomed to expecting your site will always be full. Sales were easy when there was nowhere else for your prospects to live. Many senior living sales teams focused on passive efforts to work their waitlist to meet occupancy goals. They just waited for the phone to ring.

Now the pressure is on. In an expanding competitive environment, your team needs to elevate their game as they vie with competitors who are hungry and working hard to pull prospects from considering your site to theirs.

If you begin to get your team thinking and questioning differently long before a major crisis occurs, you will develop their critical thinking skills. By teaching your team to continually ask questions and learn to be alert to the potential consequences of changing circumstances, you will be able to begin brainstorming options before you are engulfed in any enterprise-threatening crisis. Then when the next Black Swan or recession hits, as it inevitably will, these well-developed critical thinking skills among you and your staff will help you to more quickly resolve the situation or implement options you had already considered for just this situation.

The reality in today's senior living industry is everything is VUCA. Everything is uncertain about health care reform and reimbursements. With each new election cycle, you face the uncertainty of another revamping of reimbursements. Or your state and local governments may throw in a new set of regulations or rules impacting your ability to operate.

For those of you operating sites more than 20 years old, you have already been through the early startup phase in which you start to grow and fill your units and/or beds. Then the Great Recession hit. Now, for some of you – even though the market is relatively stable again – you are still at what we in strategy refer to as a "Strategic Inflection Point." An Inflection Point is the period in which you are finishing one phase of your enterprise life cycle and moving into the next phase. If you are like many older providers in our industry, you have been around long enough that you are moving from a Growth Stage to the Maturity Stage.

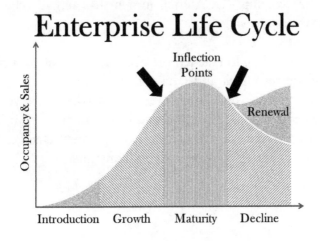

Unfortunately, for some of you who have been around for a long time, you are actually at risk of going from Maturity Stage to a Decline Stage in which your enterprise is teetering toward the edge of shutting down. Why? Because you have not modified your programming, services, resources, amenities or physical plant enough to continue to be appealing to your customers. Your competitors have so redefined market expectations that you may no longer be able to sustain the market position and occupancy you need to survive. It does happen.

We have worked in markets where competitors went out of business because overbuilding resulted in an imbalance between available units and the limited number of customers available to fill all of them. For those providers who closed, they were no longer an appealing option and their customers made the decision for them about their future. By not investing in renewing their community, the end was inevitable.

No matter where you are on the life cycle continuum, you have to learn to operate in a more strategically nimble manner. You must be able to leverage your market trends and get your teams to adjust to those changes. This is very difficult to do or everyone would be in front of it. All too often, you and everyone involved in key decision-making are too close to the situation to be objective about the magnitude of the changes that need to be made. Or, you and your team simply do not understand how much the evolving VUCA environment has actually changed the potential for your survival.

You have to be willing to take a more objective view of your situation. Tap into outside resources and advisors who can provide you with a more unbiased and clear-eyed picture of your market. Then you have to be willing to listen to what they find and recommend, even if it is hard to hear. Finally, you have to take action to implement changes that will make you more viable to your prospective consumers.

Case Study #1

The CEO and senior executives of one of the nation's largest not-for-profit multi-site senior living organizations needed information for making critical decisions and prioritizing the master-planning efforts for 12 of their campuses, including consideration of how to resolve critical issues at several distressed properties.

A comprehensive market evaluation was conducted to assess the current market position of each location. This included conducting comprehensive competitor analyses, as well as obtaining a detailed demographic assessment of the market potential for each of the various service levels offered at each site. This research provided critical insight for management and clarified the significant risks facing several locations. The information was valuable for the client team as they worked through the issues identified during the market research as critical vulnerabilities. It also established the foundation for the implementation of the priority of recommendations for change.

The CEO of this widely regarded industry leader has described this effort of engaging in such a deep level of research as "vital" to their strategic planning efforts. Since then, they have invested well over $200 million in their campuses to complete the upgrades and improvements that were identified as necessary. This ensured the survival and long-term success of their campuses in these highly competitive markets.

Chapter 3
The Strategic Impact of Evolving Demographics

While all of the nine market forces outlined earlier are important to consider, the one that has the most significant impact on senior living providers is the demographic make-up of your *local* market. National demographic trends do not impact your occupancy. What is happening in your local market demographics is what determines market need. Market need ultimately determines your occupancy potential.

Market feasibility studies for senior living assess market potential and these reports are typically used to obtain financing. The critical question for a feasibility analysis is to determine if there is a sufficient market of income qualified elderly households available in the identified market area to allow the proposed or existing units to operate at a desired level of occupancy. The primary method for determining this is to review the Market Penetration rate.

The mathematical details of calculating Market Penetration Rates are too technical a topic to be adequately discussed in this book. For our purposes here, it is more important to understand the critical variables that are used to calculated them. Essentially, Penetration Rates are a ratio that calculates the number of existing and expected senior living units (supply) relative to the number of age- and income-qualified prospects (demand) for a particular type of senior housing. The lower the rate of supply relative to demand, the less market risk for the project.

There are differences of opinion among feasibility consultants about what constitutes an acceptable Penetration Rate. Over the last decade we have seen a shift among many consultants to using higher rates to validate expanded market development. We have always taken a more conservative view of market feasibility because seniors have so many more options available to them. If we can demonstrate market potential using realistic market assumptions and a solid understanding of the competitive supply, this helps reduce the potential risk for a development or continued viability of an existing site. If those rates are unrealistically expanded to justify the financing, the risk is greater if the market does not respond as the study predicted.

It is also important to understand that feasibility studies for developing senior housing projects evaluate potential market demand by using demographics focusing on elderly population and household data for those age 75 and over. This age cohort is being used for assessing the market demand for all types of senior housing. Given the demographic shifts with the growing population of older adults, in most markets today it is easy to mathematically make nearly any project work if you use the demographic data for your feasibility analysis focusing on the combined cohorts of those adults age 75 and older.

But in reality, how many of you actually have a significant number of 75-year-old prospects moving into your senior living communities? Or even 80-year-old's? Be honest. If you are selling active adult housing or age-restricted apartments, you are likely getting a younger cohort because you are a housing alternative offering attractively priced homes with amenities such as community rooms and fitness center resources but no added services. This type of housing is doing well in most markets and there is lots of room for further expansion. Yet most of the senior living industry is focused on offering additional services such as meals, housekeeping, programming, and care to meet the needs of a much older prospect.

If you are looking at your market and expecting 75 to 84-year-olds are going to move en masse into your communities, you are likely being overly optimistic. Even those of you running independent living communities know you are highly unlikely to attract the majority of residents from the younger age cohort below the age of 80 unless you are an active adult community or are marketing a truly independent community. As a result, market feasibility studies using the younger age cohort can often overstate the current market potential, especially for housing with services and assisted living. Again, it is important to note that this is the norm for how these studies are done, but you must do a much deeper review if you want to manage your risks.

The truth is, many of the customers being served today in senior living communities, even in independent living, are actually much older than ever before. Because so many consumers delayed their decision to move due to the on-going impact from the Great Recession, they are often moving in at an older age. It is not uncommon for them to be frailer or have age-related memory issues. This often means they need more help than can be accommodated in the independent or assisted living setting or they die more quickly. For some, the cost of their care depletes their limited financial reserves at a much more rapid pace than anticipated.

Over the last decade, the average age at entry into senior living has shifted for providers in many markets. The truth is, those being served in our industry are in reality nearly a decade older than the studies being done to support much of the development activity that is now in play.

It is even more challenging when evaluating assisted living demand. The National Center for Assisted Living reports that the typical resident for assisted living is an 87-year-old woman who needs assistance with two or three activities of daily living. This makes sense because the move to assisted living is a need-based decision and someone of this age is likely to have a number of chronic health conditions. Some will have cognitive impairment and need the availability of support for medication management and/or medication administration. It is not uncommon for them to currently be living alone which can be an unsafe situation.

Yet most people do not understand that the market for independent living has also gotten older. Many providers are privately reporting to us that the average age at move in for their independent living settings now is age 85 or 86. This means there is a convergence of those moving into these independent living units being approximately the same as the age expected for a move into assisted living. This is also the typical age for those who need long-term nursing home care.

Here is the problem: The bulk of the demographic bubble in most markets of those over the age of 75 is found within the younger age cohort of people who are 75 to 79 years old. You are not going to be able to fill your units with this younger age group in the near term. Most of them are still five to ten years away from needing, or wanting, what you offer.

This younger age cohort also generally has a higher income level than the 85-year-old cohort you are realistically going to attract. Yet their incomes are buried in the data used to demonstrate that your site is feasible and can support a high fee. In most markets, when we break out the data by income and age cohort, it is shocking for our clients to see the level of income disparity.

But there is one other distressing phenomenon lurking within the demographic data. In market after market around the county, the demographics often reflect that the population age 85 and above is either showing a negative growth or at best only showing a nominal growth in this age cohort.

I was recently on-site working with one of our clients in a major Ohio metropolitan area. I have worked with this client for well over a decade.

We have spent a significant amount of time over the years carefully studying their competitors and reviewing the shifts in the local demographics to fine-tune their overall strategies, campus master planning, marketing activities, and pricing approaches.

We have watched their competitors struggle to recoup their occupancy as every new competitor opened their building. But what we observed during our recent site visit was intense and exceptionally aggressive competitive activity. The market area my client serves is absolutely overwhelmed with new construction. There are hundreds of new competitive independent and assisted living units that are either proposed or currently under construction coming into their immediate market area. Due to changes to the state's bed need methodology, nearly 500 new nursing home beds also entered their market in the last five years, including three brand new nursing home developments. It is staggering to consider the potential consequences.

In other markets across the country, there also has been an extensive amount of development occurring and the result has been a softening of occupancy for many providers. Reliable data sources such as the National Investment Center for Seniors Housing & Care (NIC) gather data from seniors housing and care providers. They confirm that occupancies are compressed throughout the nation and have generally not rebounded to the levels seen prior to the Great Recession. There are more older adults living in senior housing now, but just not enough to fill all of the units that have been built.

Without question, the current level of development activity is going to be extremely disruptive. Weak competitors will not survive, no matter what their intentions are for providing quality and loving service to their residents.

But wait ... isn't there supposed to be that significant growth in the population? Isn't that "Senior Tsunami" showing huge demographic shifts to create a massive pool of older adults who should fill every senior living community to the brim? Our findings in reviewing market after market across the nation do not support this belief. It will not be that simple. At least not in the short term.

To understand this yourself, you have to drill down deeper into the demographics of your market. Frankly, this is usually only done at a cursory level in most feasibility studies. After construction is completed, providers rarely ever go back to review how things have changed since they opened.

The bottom line is a detailed review of the local area demographics using a realistic market area for a senior living site often reflects there is only projected to be an extremely modest increase in the number of older adults age 85+ over the next five years. The growth rate is so nominal in some markets we have studied that the detailed demographic review showed there was only expected to be 20 more people aged 85+ in the market area over the next five years. Not 20% more people, but only 20 more individuals in this age cohort than are found in the market area today. It is going to be pretty hard to fill hundreds of new units in a geographic market when everyone is competing for only a sliver of the likely increase in the available prospective residents.

Remember the age cohort of 85+ is the more realistic move-in age for most senior-oriented communities with services. So, if hundreds of units are being built and only 20 more people will be of the age most likely to move in during the next five years, some providers are likely to go out of business. The new players in your market may expect this to be you.

There is no wiggle room. No matter how much you really want to lower the age to get younger seniors to move into your sites, you are highly unlikely to be exceptionally successful in achieving it if you offer access to the same services found in most communities, even those targeting a more independent senior.

Several years ago, our Ohio client asked us if we thought they should consider building more assisted living. My response was an emphatic and definite, "No!" Their market was so oversaturated with new competitors that we had identified a total of 350 new assisted living units being expected to come into their primary market area. Even with my client's market dominance, it would be risky for them to add more assisted living units. We felt they would divert significant resources away from their core business, independent living, to try to fill any new assisted living units in such a competitive situation.

Even more potentially damaging to them would be the marketing effort required to fill new assisted living units in such a highly competitive environment potentially could result in inadvertently re-positioning their predominantly independent campus as an assisted living provider. This would have had a disastrous consequence on their business model. In their marketplace, the best strategic option was to offer reasonably priced independent living and to target the active older adult who wanted to plan for their future by making a choice to enter a community offering a full continuum of care.

Our detailed demographic review in most markets also shows a higher risk level resulting from the low number of those who are age-qualified who will need assistance with the activities of daily living. That significantly narrows the market for higher level services. When overlaying the income qualifications into demand consideration, and combining it with the exceptional increase in competitive supply, any additional development can take on enormous risk or create risk for existing providers.

After our recent site visit for this client, we evaluated the impact of all the development activity we had identified two years earlier. Our review of the demand potential for senior housing absolutely confirmed that our earlier recommendation had been prudent. Assisted living occupancy was exceptionally soft and most of the providers in their market were struggling. The occupancy of one competitor, who was owned by a major national firm that you would all know, had tanked to around 50% occupancy. I was relieved that my client had heeded our advice. It is going to take years for this all to shake out in their market. Based on our findings, our planning for this client is focused on defending their market position and delivering exceptional services, resources, and a lifestyle that their residents and prospects desire.

So, what is underlying the occupancy challenges? What is driving the demographic declines in the older age cohorts in the population we are seeing within many markets? What is happening demographically that is shifting the market and increasing the competition for those prospects who are the right age for realistically moving into senior housing? It is called the Birth Dearth.

Chapter 4
The Birth Dearth

To understand the Birth Dearth, step back in time and think about those people to whom you are trying to market. When were they born? Most of the seniors you are trying to sell your services to today were born between 1930 and 1936. They were born during the era of the Great Depression.

Consider what occurred during this time period. The stock market crash in the United States occurred in October 1929. Over the next few years, the American economy was crippled. Millions of people were out of work and most families were barely surviving. Women had fewer children because they could not afford to feed the children they already had given birth to. Many infants and children born during this era died before the Depression ended. Or, they were so malnourished they either died in childhood or died before they ever reached adulthood.

The federal relief programs created to help those who were struggling did not kick in to help people until the later years of the Depression. Economic conditions eventually stabilized and food programs offering some nutritional support for children and families were implemented. By 1936, economic stimulus programs created opportunities for adults to work in "New Deal" jobs so they could once again afford to provide the basics for their families' survival. But it was a very difficult time and birth rates declined. The resulting demographic impact caused during this era created the population dip in the age cohort we are experiencing today.

In my consulting practice, we have been talking about this phenomenon with our clients for more than 15 years. We have carefully considered the potential impact of what would happen when the demographic impact of the Birth Dearth hit their markets when this age group was old enough to be the primary target market for senior living.

For most of you trying to market your campuses, if you are experiencing occupancy issues, it is highly likely you are now feeling the effects of the Birth Dearth. A detailed review of your local demographic data will likely bear this out. Combined with new competitive pressure, you have a recipe for trouble.

Consider this: if your target market was born between 1929 and 1936, you are right smack in the cohort where there is a dip in the population bubble. This means there are either fewer potential residents for you and your competitors or it is a flat population, depending on where you are located geographically. While there are a lot of variables at play, we are seeing the impact of the Birth Dearth phenomenon in market after market across the country.

What this means is you are marketing to a smaller pool of prospective residents - the older adults who actually are looking to buy what you are selling. If that was not difficult enough, now you are also competing for this smaller pool of prospects with numerous other competitive options and alternatives. When you overlay that with the income levels needed to pay your private pay rates, your true market potential can become shockingly small.

If you are marketing an assisted living community or a specific senior-focused service line, you are also competing with home health care providers because so many seniors, and their families, believe they can just stay at home, right? Seniors are told it's so easy and less expensive to just stay in their own homes. Everyone says that is the most desired option. But as a provider, you know it is not that easy or simple. Your prospective consumer does not fully understand this. Nor do their children. Even if you are offering independent living, seniors and their loved ones don't feel they need to make the move to your setting because they are "not ready" yet.

If you are experiencing challenges with your occupancy, I strongly recommend you buy the detailed demographic profile for your realistic market area. For a minimal investment, you can obtain demographic insight which will help you better understand how much your local market has shifted and what segments are projected to grow during the next five-year window. A demographic review is often the first critical step to understanding the pressure in your market.

When you get the demographics for your site, take a very close look at the detailed breakout of the adults in your market for those over the age of 75. You should look at what kind of growth or shift is occurring in the more discrete five-year age cohorts of 75 to 79, 80 to 84 and 85+. Then look at the detailed data by gender and income.

You may be quite astonished when you better understand from the objective data just how few people there may be in your market of the age that you and all your competitors are collectively chasing. This will make the challenges very clear. It will also arm you with insight to use with your boards of directors and leadership teams to discuss how to ensure you are more appealing to the limited market that is available for residence.

It has been very disconcerting for me as a consultant when I go into review markets for a highly distressed client. We often document that there are as many available senior living units in the market area as there are households with people age 85 and older!

Think about that for a minute. In some markets, there has been so much building that there is an age-restricted apartment available for every household with a senior age 85 or older who could potentially seek out services. This was without considering whether anyone had the money to afford it. It is breathtaking to see this reality flow through the data. It is also eye-opening for clients and their boards who are struggling to understand the market pressures. They often just assumed their marketing team was not working hard enough and that someone needed to be fired. We hear that all the time.

Consumers of this age have virtually unlimited choices in most markets, especially in urban areas. They have options and not all of them require moving into new housing. This is why so many providers are experiencing lower occupancies. In response, some senior living providers are just adjusting down their occupancy goals to lower levels than they used to accept to accommodate this reality. Or, they budget and spend as if they will continue to achieve an occupancy level they historically hit but which is no longer realistic. It's not hard to figure out how this "strategy" will turn out.

As we get further into this book, we are going to explore the impact of some other demographic shifts. These demographic insights may create some challenges for you -- as well as provide new opportunities.

What we also know is where there is projected growth, it is the younger cohort of older adults age 75 to 79 who are masking the real opportunity for retirement housing today. This is because when you include this younger cohort, their incomes will be higher. As a result, when you use the 75+ age as the basis for evaluating your market potential, you not only include more people who are likely not going to be your customer in the near term, but your demographic data reflects an expected higher income level than likely really exists. Remember, those age 85+ have much more limited income levels than those who are age 75 to 79.

There is even more opportunity for those pursuing development of well-designed and effectively priced active adult housing or age-restricted apartment homes with no services. But too many novice developers want to bundle more services in the hopes that they can increase the monthly rents they can charge.

Keep in mind: whenever you bundle meals or too many services into your fees, you are going to be less attractive to an independent or active older adult. There is no margin for a strategic error.

Chapter 5
The Strategic Impact of Demographics on Pricing

It is important to consider what else is impacting the incomes of those you are trying to sell to now. This income component of the demographic market force is resulting in a generation of seniors who are much different financially than those we have served in the past. This is not the GI Generation who lived through or served in World War II. The GI Generation paid off their debt and socked away a little money in the bank or under their mattress. They were teenagers or young adults during the Great Depression. They were fully cognizant of how financially devastating this period was and never want to be that afraid again. As a result, these older adults were generally debt-averse and lived within their means. They also had a defined-benefit pension plan (remember those?) which later on provided them with some income they could rely on in addition to Social Security. When they made a financial commitment, they followed through on it.

Now, the senior living industry is dealing with the Silent Generation. They are the children of those GI Generation residents we have been serving in this industry. The Silent Generation has a very different attitude toward money and debt. They were aware of the hardships of the Great Depression, but at the time were too young to be responsible for their families' welfare and survival. As they became adults, life was good again and the financial pressure was no longer a factor for their families.

In my consulting practice, we are always on the lookout for data and statistics to help us understand any shift in attitudes about debt by the Silent Generation. And we are now finding data that is creating a lot of concern. Much of the data available is a lagging indicator of how challenging this issue of debt is likely to be in the future.

Information obtained from the Federal Reserve in their Survey of Consumer Finances Chartbook which was released at the end of 2017 reflects that more than one-quarter of those over age 75 have mortgage debt (26.5%). This reflects an astonishing increase from only 6.3% of those in this age cohort having home-secured debt in 1989. Further, the average mortgage debt held by this age cohort according to the Federal Reserve study is now nearly $90,000. If you are a senior living community with an up-front entrance fee, this trend is going to have a potentially significant impact on your affordability. What is uncertain is how this trend will continue into the future.

Home-Secured Debt: Head of Household Age 75+		
Year	Percent With a Balance	Average Value of Their Debt (in 2016 dollars)
1989	6.3%	$37,000
1995	6.8%	$37,700
2007	13.9%	$84,200
2016	26.5%	$89,900
Future	??	??

SOURCE: Federal Reserve Board, *2016 Survey of Consumer Finances Chartbook*, released October 16, 2017, pages 873 and 875.

We also look at the mortgage trend data for different age cohorts in the counties in which our clients are located. Since we began doing this review a few years ago, we have seen the same type of shift into higher levels of mortgage debt documented over and over again in this data too.

Here's the kicker. This is only reviewing home-secured debt. In other reports, we are seeing increases in the use of all types of debt by those age 75+. This is installments loans, vehicle loans, credit cards, and other types of debt including education loans. Make no mistake, this shifting attitude toward expanding personal debt by the Silent Generation is going to have an impact on what these seniors are going to be able to afford and the timing of their ability to move into senior housing in the future. Yet this emerging issue is rarely discussed among senior living leaders.

Silent Generation consumers have a different attitude towards making financial commitments and following through on them. We have had many providers of new developments share with us that their pre-lease commitments to these consumers have been strong, but then they are experiencing a significant number of cancellations as their projects open. These minimal refundable pre-lease commitments, often ranging from only $500 to $1,500, are not enough skin in the game to ensure that a prospect will move in once a development opens. This can be a major financial set-back if you have to re-sell a substantial portion of your building. Silent Generation consumers are hedging their bets. For a modest financial investment, they can get their names high up on a move-in list and then wait to see what the site really has to offer once it is open. If they change their minds, as many of them do, they get all of their money back. It is no big deal to them. It is a big deal to you.

The rampant opioid addiction sweeping our country has left a number of seniors as the primary caregivers for their children and grandchildren. This has placed a financial as well as an emotional burden on many older adults as they step in to provide security for their loved ones. The other consequence of this is many Silent Generation seniors are draining their finances to meet the day-to-day needs of their extended families with little consideration for the long-term impact that reducing their net worth will have on their ability to pay for their own care if they ever need it. Their ability to enjoy the active adult lifestyle offered in the "want-based" independent senior living environment is also potentially at risk.

You should also consider the potential impact of reverse mortgages in which people pull out the equity from their homes to pay for things they want to do now or pay their current bills while living in their own home. These have the potential to deplete the value of this asset that many older adults normally use to pay for their care in their later years or to fund the entrance fee required for the senior living community they want to move into when they are finally ready.

The Silent Generation has become conditioned to believe either their children will take care of them or the government will. As a result, they are not as concerned about saving money to pay for their post-retirement years. This will have serious ramifications for senior living providers, especially as so many sites are targeting a more affluent senior household.

To complicate matters, we all know many Baby Boomers cannot or will not pay to augment the support and care of their parents. This is because many Baby Boomers are not financially very secure themselves. A number of them live in the moment or have run up their own debt. The costs of sending their children to any type of post-secondary education have skyrocketed along with health care and housing costs. They might not have the money to support themselves and their own children, much less their parents. The economic stresses have a ripple effect, especially if seniors are trying to help their younger family members go to college or buy cars and houses.

Even worse, some of those Baby Boomers are actually responsible for why their parents do not have much money in the bank. They are either spending their parent's money or manipulating their parents into spending money. I hope there is a special place in you-know-where for those people who are doing financial harm to their parents. They do it because they view their needs as taking priority and because they also think the government eventually will pay to support their parents. As a result, they don't feel like they have to be responsible with their Mom and Dad's money. Their parents can "just go on those public programs." These Baby Boomers (and sometimes their grandchildren) do not understand or care about the financial complexities they are creating for their parents.

Those of you who are involved in setting prices for your senior living community have to understand the available income of your prospect is going to become exceptionally important in the coming years. Understanding the nuances of pricing is a major challenge, and one not often considered beyond the setting of your annual fee increase. We believe this is a significant issue that providers must pay closer attention to over the next few years when they are developing their overall pricing strategy.

Here's the reality of how prices are usually established in a senior living community:

The Chief Financial Officer (CFO) says: "Our costs went up by 5% this year – our food costs went up, our utility costs went up, so therefore we need to raise our prices by 5%."

Then the Chief Executive Officer says: "That makes sense to me, this is what my CFO says we need."

Your Board members nod their heads and agree. They say: "What a great way to be fiscally responsible!"

Your marketing team is then told what the price increase will be and they are expected to sell it to the consumer.

Your residents and their families have to accept your price

increase or move somewhere else. Or they take a gamble and hope they will have enough money to pay it.

Your prospects get sticker shock and decide they can just stay at home a little longer since they don't really need what you offer yet.

Keep in mind too since the Great Recession, the incomes of most seniors have been virtually flat. In the demographic data we buy, typically their incomes have only been increasing at a very nominal level. This flat income is also echoed in Social Security increases reflecting only a 1.4% average increase in benefits between 2013 to 2019. The Social Security cost of living increase for 2019 of 2.8% is double the benefit increase in any of the prior five years. Yet how many of you have had price increases during this period that have annually been 2%, 3% or even 7% as we recently saw in one urban market?

There are real market consequences to setting your price increases well above the level of the annual Social Security cost of living increase. If you are continually increasing your prices above those rates, the impact of the compounded increases over the years can really cause problems. All too often, the impact of the trajectory of increasing your rates compounds over time and results in what we call an Affordability Gap.

Think about what is really happening to the incomes in your target market. In recent years, the Social Security increase has been very nominal or non-existent. Then when you look at the detailed demographic data you also will see nominal annual increases projected in the incomes of your consumers.

In nearly all of the markets we study, those increases have been at best 1.5% to 2.0% annually since the Great Recession. This means your consumer's incomes are increasing at only 2.0% or less per year, while at the same time you are increasing your prices between 3% and 5%. The math just doesn't work.

When you increase your prices at a more rapid rate it will often shift your prices to a level well above what your target consumers can afford to pay. If this happens, you are going to get in trouble. At some point, the velocity of your annual pricing increases will outpace your consumers' incomes, resulting in an Affordability Gap. Fewer and fewer of those in your desired target market are likely to be able to afford your site over time. Your market potential will drop as you become less affordable.

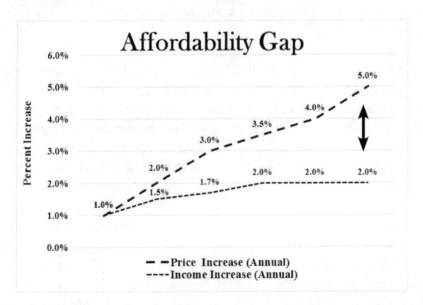

Suddenly, people who should be living in your senior communities cannot afford you or they develop a psychological barrier to affordability. This means the influence of income on your pricing strategy is a powerful market force impacting the demographic potential that you must deeply consider.

In some markets, competitors (and maybe even you) are offering price discounts and rent-locks for several years to get people to move into their buildings. This is happening because providers are finding their prices are too high for the local market. They are re-framing their price points to try to find the sweet spot where consumers are willing to say yes.

If you are like most providers who were built over a decade ago, you were likely affordable to your market at the time of your original market feasibility study. But in the intervening years, if you accelerated prices above 2% each year, you may have inadvertently priced yourself out of your market. This means the compounded impact of your higher annual price increases have so narrowed the available market of those who can afford you that there are no longer enough prospects actually available in your local area to keep you full at the income level these price points require.

We see this phenomenon all the time: lovely senior living communities that are no longer financially feasible to enough of the consumers they want to sell to. This is even further compounded because most of the new communities being built are targeting a higher-end consumer. This is not a challenge for affordable senior living communities targeting households with limited incomes, but the pressure is on for the more affluent senior.

When we completed this type of review for an upscale senior community we worked with, it turned out the compounded impact of increasing prices without considering the market consequence had catastrophic results. The review showed the client was now only affordable to 9% of the households age 75+ living within their market area. It is pretty hard to fill a building when so few can afford you. It was even harder for them since new competitors had entered their market. These new competitors were a more affordable option even when targeting an affluent group of seniors and they were capturing residents from my client's prospect list. The fee savings gave prospects more peace of mind about their long-term finances or they were using the savings for travel and other experiences. The updated market feasibility analysis of their affordability was a major reality check for everyone.

For years our industry has served older adults on both ends of the income spectrum. Housing and service options are either focused on upscale and expensive offerings to a more affluent resident or they are focused on affordable options for low-income seniors. There are generally few providers focused on meeting the needs of the middle-income senior market. Reasonably priced private pay options are an important consideration that all providers should review as they look to meet the needs of their community. The market for these seniors might be even bigger than you expect!

The other part of the demographic shift that is occurring for some of you is that your geographic market area boundaries for who you attract to your sites may be changing at the same time as the demographics shift. We always carefully review the actual target market area for our clients. Frequently when we are involved with a turnaround client, their marketing teams will tell us, "Our market area is XYZ." At one point in time, this might have been a true statement. But not today. In market after market, we typically see a geographic shrinkage of our client's market area. This is most often due to the impact of the entrance of new competitive alternatives.

Client teams are rarely adept at looking at (or admitting) how much their market area draw patterns are shifting and changing over time. This type of analysis requires detailed data review and looking at shifts over different time horizons. They have other pressing priorities commanding their attention each day. Or they are overly optimistic that they will be able to be successful in expanding the market draw again.

Every time a new competitor enters your market, you are at risk for a market area redefinition. Every time a new roadway is constructed, the traffic patterns in a region change. Closures of major retail centers or employers not only impact demographic shifts in your immediate site area, but they also can result in your site having a market draw pattern that is significantly different from your historical one. Pulling unique demographic datasets using various market area boundary definitions can help you assess the potential risks if your market area changes.

In more than three decades of consulting to the senior living industry, I have never seen a client who has had a stagnant market area definition. Never. Something always shifts and those shifts can be consequential to your enterprise survival.

Sometimes your initial feasibility study was overly optimistic about where you would draw your residents from or was just plain wrong. Frequently the market area used for a feasibility study is a best guess, which may not be accurate once operation begins. Often the actual experience of a new development shows a much narrower market area geography than what was used in the feasibility study that financed it. This can be devastating to your occupancy if your market area is different than the one used for financing. We have seen this happen. It is much more common than you might think. The consequences can be substantial.

A combination of factors will influence the market determination of a senior living community. In particular, the key determinants of market definition include the suitability and appeal of the concept, the site location in terms of market orientation, accessibility, and current patterns being experienced by other area senior housing facilities. If it is an existing site, the most important determinant is the current experience of the senior living provider. The historical address of prior origin of your residents should be evaluated to understand how your market draw patterns are shifting and changing over time.

Consumers will generally not move that far away from their home unless they have a pull factor like an adult child living elsewhere or they are going back to a community in which they have strong ties. These ties can be based on where they grew up, went to college, raised their children, served in the military, etc. So, despite having large ZIP Codes, suburbs or other communities nearby your site, the reality is you may not actually be able to draw enough residents from them to meet, or sustain, your occupancy goals.

In rural or smaller communities, local ties are significant and these psychological ties can become barriers to older adults moving even a few miles down the road. In some rural locations, towns are building small limited-scale senior living developments to retain their older adults. Meanwhile, peripheral larger cities that have historically captured these seniors now find that they have been boxed out from their traditional market area draw patterns. This is because these smaller provider sites are now capturing the edges of the market area. Yet most will still continue to include these distant communities in their market area boundary even if they can no longer document residents coming from them.

Market area definition is exceptionally hard to develop with accuracy unless you objectively study it. The key is to really hone into the local market to understand how it functions. This includes reviewing retail trade patterns, media market distribution areas, major church congregational patterns, local community inter-relationships, and the experience of other senior living sector competitors. It is essential to consider whether your market area definition is contracting. Then you can determine if there are any options for expanding it again or determining how you will deal with the consequences if you cannot.

Unfortunately, most feasibility studies only use a cursory review to develop the market draw used for the demand analysis. It is just the nature of the work. Few developers are willing to invest in conducting a more detailed review of the market. Most are just looking for the cheapest study they can buy so they can get their financing approved. Leaders who understand and value deeper analyses will invest in the value offered by a more comprehensive review to understand all their potential demographic, market, and financial risks.

When was the last time you really looked objectively at your market area definition? Or matched it to an updated review of the demographics? What new demographic trends and patterns are occurring within your resident and prospective resident data? You might be operating off an older set of insights and assumptions about your market area than the actual market potential you now have.

Take the time to do a deeper dive review of your customer base and their origins. Track the location of the adult children of your residents. This will help you better assess your market draw. Keep your updated target market information in mind and match geographic market area boundaries with a review of the demographics for the area so you will know how those factors are working together. If you are having occupancy challenges, you might be in for a real shock when you dive deeper into studying your market area draw patterns and then combining that with a demographic review.

We have seen a variety of distressed properties in recent years that were built after using unrealistic market area definitions and Penetration Rates that overstated their market potential The consultants who did these studies said they had just done a "preliminary" assessment, not a full market feasibility study. When challenged by clients who are now struggling, these consultants told them they should not have used this "limited review" for financing. The client did not know the difference. Regardless of intent, these studies were used for investment and the lack of depth of the study was playing out in operations that were in deep trouble.

Other times we see cookie cutter studies that were inexpensively done because the developer just wanted to obtain financing and that was all the bank, lender or investor needed to see. We recently talked with a financier about a study that had been submitted to them for consideration of the development of a new independent housing with services and assisted living project. This feasibility study used demographics for the analysis focusing on the total population age 65+ without any further analytical refinement of the older age cohorts. The study did not even have any income breaks for the age cohorts, just an overall income level for all households in the market area. Frankly, it was a relief to learn the lender passed on financing the development. There were simply too many unanswered questions about the market.

All of these variables and demographic intricacies are deeply inter-twined to provide you with an understanding of how realistic your market opportunity really is. Going forward, the impact of market area definition on feasibility will take on much more significance. You need to track and review detailed information to manage your potential risk. Information is power and gives you the insight you need to anticipate problems long before they impact your occupancy. That advance insight gives you time to determine how you will need to respond so you can sort out your options.

Case Study # 2

A developer was considering the potential opportunity for an active adult housing development in New Mexico. They needed information to assist them in evaluating the assumptions they were using for their master planning process. The developer wanted to make sure they were creating a community that would match the market needs and expected consumer desires for such a site. They also needed to determine if their revenue projections using the prices they hoped to charge were realistic for the local market.

Extensive research was conducted to evaluate the availability of other competitive alternatives to meet the housing needs of age 55+ empty nesters. This provided the developer with insight into the size of units that should be offered and was used to analyze the market potential for the development considering various price points. This scenario analysis approach also allowed them to evaluate profitability options. Information was obtained to gauge the New Mexico community's reputation as a destination retirement area for seniors. This research also provided additional ideas on how to develop a campus that would have broad market appeal. The competitive insight provided the developer with clarity that some of their initial assumptions about the design of the project were out of sync with local market expectations. They were able to retool their campus design using this market intelligence.

Using the information gathered, the developer was able to assess the viability of their initial development plan. They recalculated their projected profitability in light of the new market information.

Chapter 6
The Strategic Impact of Competition

Another major market force impacting senior living demand today is the dynamic of extensive competition exploding in many markets. Years ago in this industry there were basically two kinds of congregate housing for seniors: independent living and nursing homes. Then this "new" concept called assisted living began to emerge in the mid-1980s. At the time, I was working in the consulting division of one of the nation's largest CPA firms doing market feasibility studies for senior living. I was selected to be a part of the firm's team that developed the analytical parameters for how market feasibility studies for assisted living are conducted. Little has changed in the methodology in the intervening years.

But today, the boundaries around the concept of independent and assisted living is so smudgy that frequently no one understands it – especially the consumer. In recent years it has become exceptionally difficult to figure out what our clients' local competitors are actually offering to prospects. This is another outgrowth of the impact of the Great Recession.

In many markets around the country, providers are promoting themselves as "independent living" when in truth they are actually operating as assisted living communities offering a heavy emphasis on assistance by bundling meals and services to get higher price points.

Some have a design that requires residents to receive three meals a day because there are no kitchens in the units. Yet they are being marketed as "independent" living. We see this all the time. In truth, for most of these providers, "independent living" is just their base assisted living level with the primary services included being three meals, housekeeping, some utilities, activities and the potential to add home care or healthcare services for an added fee as the residents age in place.

Just because you call it "independent living" does not mean a truly independent resident will choose to live in your community or be willing or able to pay you for extra services they don't believe they need yet. This smudgy approach does offer older seniors who are frail, but too proud to admit they need help, with an opportunity to say to others that they are residing in independent living so they won't be embarrassed. Unfortunately, it is confusing and usually ends up skewing the resident mix to those who are older, frailer and/or somewhat cognitively impaired.

Independent living providers are so desperate to stay full they are trying to meet everyone's needs. They are bundling many services into their monthly fees. Now they are operating more like assisted living communities. Those offering services are charging a base monthly fee plus the costs for additional care.

Good luck to your prospects and their families in figuring out how much these services are actually going to cost them each month. Often these prices are based on the admission "assessment" and adjusted upward at different intervals. Are you crystal clear with your prospects what the monthly fee is going to be at admission and what determines how it may change? Your prospects are likely confused. Frankly, I am often confused too when I am studying competitors in a market, and I am an exceptionally sophisticated consumer of senior living services.

We even see providers who offer independent and assisted living calling themselves "continuing care" communities or who proudly promote they offer a "full continuum of care." While that sounds good in your marketing materials, you really cannot be considered a true full continuum without offering nursing home care on your site too. In some markets, to be considered a full continuum, you also have to offer hospice services and respite resources to families.

Keep in mind, each market is different, but the basics of a full continuum require at least the three major levels of care: independent living, assisted living, and nursing home care. We have facilitated focus groups of the consumers you are trying to market these limited continuum communities to who are very savvy about what services, resources, and options should be included. Trust me, they notice what is missing and they can become very vocal in talking about how it impacts their decision.

When we are reviewing competitors for our clients, we have to be very careful to fully understand what they are promoting and how they are actually providing services when marketing to prospects. Marketing messages alone no longer can be relied upon. Frankly, your marketing message may be skewed too.

I once saw a website for a provider who touted they offered a full continuum of care. Our further review clarified that they offered long-term care beds and a post-acute care unit with short-term rehabilitation beds. In this competitor's mind, this was a full continuum of care. But this phrasing would be exceptionally confusing for a consumer or their family. I know I was confused before I did a deeper dive into what they offered.

We now see efforts in the industry to rebrand continuing care retire-ment communities (CCRC's) into life plan communities (LPC's). Regardless of the alphabet soup of letters used, the consumer is confused. This is especially challenging when some states license providers specifically using the CCRC designation and the providers are trying to market using the LPC label. We are also occasionally seeing informal CCRCs emerging with operators of independent living collaborating with nearby assisted living and nursing homes to create these types of communities without the overarching operational control or ownership of a single entity. It is still unclear how well these arrangements will compete.

Honestly, even with our deep experience, it is often extremely challenging for us to figure out exactly what competitors are doing when we enter a new market. Sometimes it can even be difficult to understand what our own clients are offering to their local market.

We have to invest a lot of time into pulling the markets apart so we can understand the various providers serving them and where they each fit. Imagine how challenging it is for a typical consumer and their family.

If someone like me who is a highly sophisticated and experienced consultant in senior living has trouble initially figuring out what you are offering, trust me, your consumers are even more confused. When was the last time you did an objective marketing audit to review all aspects of your promotional and sales approaches? This can be an exceptionally helpful effort, especially if combined with a comparison to your competition.

Do you really know what your competitors are truly offering? All too often, we find clients have outright dismissed local providers as not being directly competitive only for us to discover in our research with key referral sources that they are much more of a competitor than anyone on the client team had ever considered. This usually happens when client teams are relying on a dated or biased view of the local market. Client teams are focused inward. Competitive intelligence requires an outward and objective view.

Often, I will say to a client, "Did you know competitor XYZ is doing this, this, and this? Did you know that competitor ABC now has relationships with here, here, and here?"

Nearly every time I ask questions like this, the client team had no idea. It is not because they don't want to consider the competition, it's just that they are too busy with their daily job responsibilities. Or, they had already dismissed the competitor and did not feel they needed to pay attention to it.

Don't be hard on them. They are doing day-to-day operations, delivering client services, and dealing with families struggling with aging transitions. Doing a thorough competitive analysis is a separate analytical skill, and it is not one most of your teams are typically prepared for or properly trained to do.

Take a look at your competitive market with a fresh set of eyes. Look carefully at what your competitors say they offer and compare it to what they actually offer. This will help you to better understand who they serve and how they fit in meeting the needs of seniors in your marketplace.

Your competitors are changing your market relationships too. For instance, you may have historically been strong in appealing to people of a certain faith or local church. But if your residents have aged in place long enough, you are probably providing faith services on your own site for your residents' convenience. Your current residents are no longer going back to their home parish for an occasional Mass or worship service. This now limits your visibility in those local churches.

Here is what your competitors are doing now: they are driving their buses and vans to those local churches that you have always relied on as a feeder for your residents. When they bring their residents back to the local church for a service, other seniors and adult children attending those churches see your competitor's van (and the sign on their vehicle). They will realize they have friends or acquaintances living in those competitors and they have the ability to ask them directly how they like living with this provider. This creates opportunities for prospects you might have considered to be yours to begin considering these other competitive options.

In our experience, people at those churches say, "Well, Vivian lives at Wonderful Senior Living Community and Mary lives at Wonderful

Senior Living Community. I always thought I was going to be at Saint Whatever Senior Living, but I am going to go look at where Vivian and Mary live because they told me how happy they are there."

This can become really important because you may have fallen off the radar for your prospects. You and your team are so focused on serving your residents on your site, you have taken for granted that your existing referral relationships will continue. These relationships will end unless you work to keep them. Just like any relationship, it takes a continued investment to keep them alive and active.

Step back and try to understand what is going on within your competition and consider how the changes in your competitive market-place may impact your on-going viability and sales opportunities. If you don't have time, seek out an advisor who has deep experience in senior living to do the research for you.

Also don't forget your competitors frequently won't tell you the whole truth, even if they are your "friendlies" – you know, the ones you always call when you are doing your annual market intelligence and share basic information with each other. These are those calls where your team asks what their occupancy is and gets a little insight on their current pricing. You often hear they are full, don't you? Well, they probably are full of something but it's likely not residents.

It is really much tougher in many markets than most people are willing to admit – especially for those of you located in larger metropolitan areas. They may be telling you they are "full" when what "full" means is actually based on what they have currently staffed. They may have had to informally remove beds from service because of an inability to fill them or because they cannot recruit enough staff to operate them. Or they may be struggling to get residents because the apartments in their 30-year-old building are too small to be sold to today's demanding senior living prospect. You also have to pay close attention to their shifting unit mix as they may be consolidating their small units, thus resulting in fewer units being marketed and available on their site. Consolidating small units to create a more desirably sized unit has been a game changer for many older communities. Re-tooling your site and unit mix might be the first step to getting back into the game.

Unfortunately, because there has been so much competitive development activity in many markets and the demographic pressure results in fewer available consumers, many providers are struggling with occupancy. As a result, your sales teams are desperate to fill your sites. They are promoting everything and the kitchen sink to get people into your units. Anyone who will say "yes" is fair game. This is how the "smudgy" marketing impacts your site. This also makes it increasingly difficult to determine if a site is independent living, assisted living or some sort of hybrid.

Do you provide one meal a day? Can your residents add meals as desired? Do you include three meals a day and call it independent living? Do you offer units with a full kitchen? Or is your "independent" unit really just a room with a sink, small refrigerator and microwave? If you are promoting your higher care resource with the kitchenette as independent living, your site may turn off the traditional independent living consumer who is looking for more of a lifestyle-based housing option.

What are you really offering to your prospects? How does it appeal to your market? Trying to be everything to everyone may have made your offerings so confusing that you don't appeal to anyone. Frequently we often have to physically go into the apartments of our client's competitors to be able to discern what it really is and how it competes in the market.

We are also observing another issue emerging in market after market when communities are not full: they start scrambling to admit those on Elderly Waiver and other social service financing programs. These can vary from state to state. Those who are covered by these programs are usually very easy sales.

If you are pressuring your sales team to fill your apartments, they will look for the easiest way to get warm bodies into your units. While filling your building with too many Waiver residents may meet your mission, it can also have significant financial consequences. Let me explain what accepting Waivers can really mean to what you create in your senior living environment.

When you introduce a resident into your site who is benefiting from these types of financing programs, you are likely accepting people who have complex health care needs, are younger with mental illness, or both. This can create real challenges for your site.

If you are admitting residents with more complex care needs, you will likely need more staff to provide the additional care. It is not uncommon to end up in a situation in which you now have an occupied assisted living unit or nursing home bed, but you are usually not getting fully reimbursed by the government program for all of the costs associated with the care you need to provide these residents. It becomes a costly admission.

If you are admitting more residents with mental illness, you may place your team members at risk. Younger residents with psychiatric issues may also make your site less attractive to your traditional senior prospects and their families. We have seen that happen in more than one market.

A few years ago, we worked on a turnaround for a senior living community in Seattle whose previous marketing director felt if there was an empty assisted living unit, they should just fill it with someone covered by the Medicaid Waiver program. This approach resulted in them getting a short-term boost in occupancy and a bit of revenue. But this marketing director never considered the longer-term consequence to their site. Those who were coming in under this program were exactly as described earlier: younger with complex comorbidities and serious mental health issues. These issues were not garden-variety depression, but serious mental illnesses such as schizophrenia and bipolar disorder.

This was seriously impacting their profitability and had created a less than desirable situation for their other residents.

Yes, bringing in these younger high-need residents gets an empty unit filled; but keep in mind these residents won't be like your typical assisted living resident who cycle out of your community through transition to higher care or death within a 12 to 36-month window. They will likely be with you for a much longer time. Years in fact. And their limited income at move-in ensures they will always qualify for a low-income program.

If you take in one 62-year-old with complex medical needs and mental illness, then another one, and then another one and then another, sooner rather than later you will have a very bifurcated group of residents living in your building. You may end up with 60% to 80% of your residents being made up of the typical 85 to 87-year-old frail women who are now living with a significant group of younger residents who are mentally ill and/or have complex medical conditions. This can get out of hand quickly if you are not carefully monitoring who is being admitted to your site and how many are slotted into each financial program.

You may think this is an overstatement, but we see it all the time. I recently studied a nursing home in a rural community that had embarked on an even more unusual approach to trying to stay full. They were providing services to young adults from a nearby major metropolitan area who had been court-ordered to be admitted for chemical dependency treatment requiring a skilled nursing placement. Most of these young clients had both substance abuse and mental health issues. The older adults living here were from the local community. They were now mixing with these younger short-term residents. Staff dismissed any concerns by telling our secret shopper the older adults "don't mind" mixing with the younger chemical dependent patients because they will "help the seniors out a lot by picking up things." This created a very unstable and transient environment for those older adults who needed long-term care placement. But they and their families had limited options unless they were willing to move to another nearby town.

The other consequence of taking too many residents on the various Waiver programs is you end up having to charge your private-pay residents more. This results in cost shifting to pay for this uncompensated care to your 87-year old female resident. She is now not only paying for her care, but also subsidizing these other residents to help make-up your budget shortfall to cover the cost of their care. No one ever talks about this, but it is true. You might be able to stabilize your price increases to a more modest and affordable level for your private pay market if you don't have to cover all of these uncompensated costs. This is sobering food for thought.

Also adding to the complexity is that it becomes even more difficult for your team to program and serve two completely different resident groups. This becomes a very problematic dynamic to work through as these two resident groups are often from different generations. These generational differences can be profound in their interest in activities, music, movie preferences, basic communication styles, and food preferences. This makes things much harder on your staff.

As a consultant, I prefer to come and visit competitors doing what I call, "coming in the front door." In those circumstances, you know who I am and that I am working for another identified local provider. We often get push back from some providers who do not want to talk with us. Honestly, it is in your best interest to talk with me and the other consultants like me who are working on studies in your area. You can control the tour and what you tell me. If you do not let me in the front door, we must get the insight we need another way – often this is by secret shopping. When we have to secret shop you, it ends up as a waste of your sales team's time. Further, it results in only a one-sided conversation where we get insight about you. By agreeing to meet with me, you get the opportunity to talk with me about what I am finding as I am reviewing your market. In return for meeting with me, I will often share market intelligence tidbits or demographic insight because those meeting with me have been generous in sharing with me and showing me their community.

In our research, we are finding occupancy challenges occurring among providers in many markets around the nation. Sometimes these providers are highly experienced players you would never in a million years think would have sites that are struggling. In fact, some of these sites are on the tipping point because of the critical insights you are reading about so far in this book. I have had some highly-experienced senior level executives operating well-known multi-site senior living communities tell me privately in the past year that as many as half or more of their properties are technically under water. It is happening all over the nation. Perhaps this is even happening to you.

Case Study #3

A troubled Illinois-based lifecare retirement community was acquired by an experienced senior housing operator. The independent living units of the campus had never enjoyed full occupancy in its 15-year history. Campus marketing staff blamed the occupancy issues on community perceptions of the financial challenges the campus had experienced nearly a decade earlier. Management needed to turn the situation around and wanted to know what the real reasons were for the inability of the campus to fill. To complicate matters, management had recently acquired 30 acres of property adjacent to the campus for development of townhome units.

Community and customer perceptions clarified the previous financial issues of the prior owner were no longer a factor impacting the current occupancy issues. Extensive research determined the apartment units were not filling due to the undesirability of the unit size in comparison to newer competitive options available. The site's highly bundled pricing package including two meals per day and other services made the independent living units much less appealing to the healthier and more active senior they were targeting. Further, the true market area draw was coming from a much narrower geographic area than anyone realized.

The strategic market analysis revealed it would be impossible to fill the campus units from within the highly competitive market unless more effective marketing efforts were employed to attract residents from a slightly broader geographic area. The market review determined this was possible and reasonable. Coaching was done with the marketing director to help increase her understanding of how to truly capitalize on these opportunities. The market opportunity analysis for the proposed townhome units provided the client with information used to develop pricing strategies, unit sizing, and amenities.

Recommendations were identified to change the service package and programming to make the campus more appealing. A major renovation was recommended to make the campus much more competitive within their local market. The marketing efforts of the campus were redesigned based on insight gathered from the market. The independent living units and the new 30-acre townhome development were effectively marketed and have been filled.

Chapter 7
Curb Appeal

For those of you leading mature senior living communities, keep in mind that while curb appeal is important, it is not everything to your customers. It is a factor in how consumers make their decisions, but it is not the only factor. I have been in markets where comfortable, but not fancy, communities were operating at full capacity. There were unique reasons they were able to overcome their lack of high-end curb appeal. They were carefully priced, hired staff who provided a wonderful level of engagement, and offered services such as meals and activities that matched the residents' expectations, tastes, and budget.

Attractive settings often seduce families. Few of them have any experience in evaluating senior housing, so they evaluate locations based on what they can see. Your sales staff will have people coming in to tour your site who just toured a brand-new community down the street which has decorative wallpaper, gorgeous artwork, and plush furniture in the common areas. By comparison, your site might be showing its age and at first glance, your physical plant does not come across as modern. But don't be dismayed. Curb appeal is not the only thing that matters.

The impact of curb appeal really hit home for me when I was engaged to evaluate the turnaround opportunities for a client. Part of our work required us to evaluate the potential impact of a new $200 million big gorilla competitor that was going to come online just outside the client's primary market area. We knew this gorilla would be directly competing with us for residents.

Honestly, I was extremely concerned my client would not be able to survive going up against this competitor once they opened their new campus. My client's campus was nearly 30 years old and they had not invested significantly in maintaining the cosmetic appeal of their physical plant. They had invested in their roof, windows, and elevators. These are the things you need to do, but they do not influence how a prospect views you on a sales tour.

But it turned out the $200 million gorilla only had curb appeal. While they were an experienced operator, they entered the market with a know-it-all attitude. This attitude resulted in them misreading the marketplace. That developer had completely misunderstood the market potential and the local culture. They ended up building a development that did not make sense in the market. Their price points were obscenely high and their service delivery when they opened was abysmal. Their prospective consumers did not want what they had created because there were no nursing home beds on site and prospects did not view them as offering a full continuum of care even though they were marketing the site this way. Those prospects who considered it shared their views among their peers and the word of mouth on the street was harsh. This insight was candidly and emphatically shared with us in focus groups we conducted for our client.

The leadership of the gorilla site blamed their low occupancy and lack of consumer interest on the Great Recession. The truth was they had made a mess of everything. Their campus layout and design were dreadful. Only one of their independent living buildings was even connected to their central commons area and it was attached to the assisted living building. Seems like no big deal, right? But these independent residents had to walk through the assisted living building to go to dinner or the exercise area. The building locations should have been flipped, right? Especially since the assisted living building was essentially a stand-alone operation. The rest of the residents living in detached buildings on this

80-acre campus had to navigate the midwestern weather patterns by walking outside to take advantage of the site's common areas.

Plus, the whole development was focused on positioning them as an upscale and very pretentious campus. Their prices reflected this. They were priced way beyond the market's ability and willingness to bear these costs. Even those prospects who had the necessary financial resources balked at paying prices this high, especially when this site was not perceived to be offering a full continuum of care.

This developer put all their money into the glitz of their common areas. They had impressive artwork on the walls and even an art studio. Yet when you looked at the resident apartments, in their zeal to be different, the developer had not considered the practical realities for the older adults who would be living in them. The granite countertops in the kitchen were gorgeous, but the cupboards were too high for an older adult who had lost some height or who had any mobility issues impacting their range of motion in their shoulders. Cupboards under the counter did not have pull out drawers. Those little things mean a lot to an older adult who is trying to maintain their independence.

My client and I recognized the gorilla's curb appeal could be a competitive challenge. We carefully considered the demographic impact of various pricing approaches in a very detailed manner. This allowed us to analyze the income level of the older adults in the market area so the site could maximize the pool of prospects who could afford their campus. We conducted focus groups to assess the effectiveness of sales messaging and to gain input about how they viewed the client's services and resources relative to the gorilla and other key competitors. We completed a comprehensive marketing audit of their promotional plan and looked for new opportunities for more effective marketing outreach activities. We developed a re-focused branding strategy to better emphasize the well-researched marketing messages. We also worked with the board to prioritize plans for major campus renovations to upgrade and enhance their common areas and resident amenities.

The local market rejected the gorilla and they eventually filed for bankruptcy. The gorilla then re-calibrated their pricing by making huge adjustments to drop their price points and entrance fees. But they did not effectively address the unevenness of their service levels, even though they are still priced at a very high level.

When I was back in the market several years after their bankruptcy, I was able to confirm that the gorilla had only reached 75% occupancy, despite cutting their prices by 25%. It was a complete disaster for them. They have been marketing this campus for a decade and they still have units available that have never had anyone living in them! My client adjusted to the changing market, identified and then zeroed in on their sweet-spot to be competitive. Today they are doing exceptionally well financially, have made superb renovations to their campus, and are operating at full occupancy with a long wait list.

Physical amenities in your units can differentiate you in the market. Recently I attended an open house for a new community which was competing with another of my clients. I was pleased to see they had included mini-refrigerators in their assisted living units which had been raised up from the floor to make them easier to use. It is the livability of the units which makes a difference. Those are the little touches that have a big impact on your residents and future residents.

Hospitality is also what your consumers are craving. Having a hospitality mindset causes you to understand what your consumer wants and how your team executes on that mindset every day. Now I do not mean you should offer hospitality to the point where you are doing every little thing for your residents. This will make them dependent and you will likely have to absorb the costs of all the services because they want it but won't (or cannot) pay for it.

What I mean by hospitality is you create a friendly and welcoming environment. You create an environment they can truly call their home. You create a sense of community. You know their names, their families, their friends, and their faiths. You know their favorite foods and carefully observe, and appropriately react to, how they are adjusting to their new senior lifestyle. In other words, you "manage by walking around" rather than sitting in an office all day.

You can overcome much of the lack of curb appeal at your site if your residents feel they are cared about and believe they matter to you. Too many of the senior living communities I have toured in the past few years that have glitzy exteriors and beautiful lobbies have no heart or any real connection to hospitality or service. Nor do they have any real connection to their residents or the local community.

When you think about your curb appeal, look for the smaller, incremental changes you can make. Consider some of the cosmetic enhancements you can make that don't require hiring an interior designer or an extensive renovation. Start to recognize some of the subtle differences in the psychology of the consumers you are now serving. How does this potentially impact the need to modernize your common areas? Consider what the services and activities you offer mean to the health and well-being of your residents. Be sure to engage them in re-shaping your living environment. After all, it is their home.

Case Study #4

The Board of Directors of a 20-year old, nationally-accredited continuing care retirement community in the Northeastern region of the United States needed to understand the reasons why a recent $20 million expansion of the independent living portion of their campus was not filling.

A comprehensive strategic market analysis provided critical insight into the changing competitive environment and an assessment of how well they were positioned to compete effectively within this changing marketplace. A careful review of their pricing strategies assessed the challenges created by pressures being experienced in the local real estate market conditions and the changing economics of area retirees. A strategic planning retreat involving the organization's board and senior management reviewed the shifts in the market and candidly discussed the available options for rethinking pricing strategies and physical plant renovations.

A subsequent comprehensive marketing audit evaluated the effectiveness of their promotional efforts and determined a variety of adjustments needed to be made in positioning the site, especially in considering the messaging and photographic images used in their marketing materials. This was vital given how a new competitor was positioning their site to prospects. This review included a conversation with staff to review their operational focus and need to be more responsive to the shifts observed in the competitive market. This review also determined significant investments needed to be made to the site's physical plant in order to remain competitive.

By being open to participating in a deeper review of their local market, engaging in a frank discussion of the changes they needed to make, and then implementing a cohesive strategy to address the challenges identified, this senior living provider was successful in achieving a complete turnaround of this organization within less than six months. Significant construction over the next several years invested more than $10 million in new and expanded resident amenities. It is now considered to be the premier senior living community within its primary market area and it is fully occupied.

Chapter 8
The Strategic Impact of Health Care

Chronic conditions tie to the demographics of your market. They will vary by age, race and ethnicity. Each type of chronic condition creates potential new opportunities for service depending on the unique age make-up and ethnic diversity found in your local market area. There are typically different rates per thousand of population or percentages of age groups experiencing various types of chronic conditions. These are called Prevalence Rates. Understanding your market's demographic variables when combined with utilizing Prevalence Rates can help you anticipate who will need and use your services.

Closely review your demographics and Prevalence Rates so you can determine if you could incorporate the management of a specific chronic condition such as dementia or diabetes into your services. You can use this type of data to explore opportunities to see is there a new sub-sector you had not previously considered that might create a new service line for you. This might help you start appealing to a younger component of the population age 75 and above. We are observing an increase in some chronic conditions due to obesity and poor lifestyle choices. Is there an opportunity for you to be the "healthier lifestyle" leader in your community?

Functional limitations are changing too. As older consumers are trying to take control themselves of improving their health, in some markets we have seen a decline in those with some functional limitations in either their Instrumental Activities of Daily Living (IADLs) or their Activities of Daily Living (ADLs). Functional limitations impact the need for higher care services such as home health care, assisted living, and nursing home beds.

Nursing home utilization is declining in many markets around the nation. The increased availability of assisted living facilities is a more desirable consumer preference for the delivery of care, especially for the private pay market. In the future, technology may have an even greater impact on the potential need for certain types of providers. As consumers grow more comfortable with the use of technology for distributing medications or to manage their chronic conditions, this market force may reduce the need for long-term care facilities or shorten the length of stay even further, which will further impact nursing home utilization. Are you prepared to compete in this environment?

There is another phenomenon Chris Anderson, editor-in-chief of *Wired Magazine*, wrote about in his book entitled, "The Long Tail." While his book was written focusing on the impact of technology, the concept applies very well to the senior living sector. Roughly 80 percent of what you do will meet everybody's needs in your site. But then there is the "Long Tail" which says for each consumer there are going to be one or two unique elements you offer which will be the reason they pick you or stay with you. What is important to them, beyond the common basics, will be different depending on the type of facility you operate or level of care you provide.

So as a leader in your marketplace, you must stay close enough to your consumers and their families to understand what it is they need from you, what it is they want from you, and what it is they will pay for. Always keep in mind: you need to be paid for what you do and what you offer. Your services have value. The challenge will be to price them at a level reflecting all your costs and within the realistic range of what your consumers can and will pay.

For those of you operating nursing home beds, there are many shifts happening that are now impacting this level of care and its utilization. For some providers, this is resulting in a rude awakening and major pressure.

If you look back at nursing home utilization rates in the 1980s, many of you were operating nursing homes that had consistently full beds. You were successful in capturing a significant portion of the target market available in your communities for those over the age of 85. These residents were often lovely elderly women who needed a long-term custodial environment and some support. Of course, no one wanted to be in a nursing home and families had enormous anxiety about "putting" their loved ones there. We all know families that splintered irrecoverably when siblings fought over these decisions.

Today, that same 85-year-old prospective resident is now the primary target market for assisted living. Frankly, assisted living is a much more palatable environment for them and their families. This is especially true for those who have historically been targeted by the private pay nursing home market. As a result, nursing bed utilization has dropped significantly all around the country. Providers have adjusted by adding short-term post-acute rehabilitation beds and services. Some have shifted to providing long-term care to those with complex medical conditions and multiple co-morbidities. It is not uncommon for these residents to be younger and/or on Medicaid.

What's happening is your consumers are choosing other alternative venues such as care suites, assisted living or home health to meet their higher-level care needs. Assisted living providers are trying to hang onto their residents longer. Some are pushing the boundaries of their services to the nursing home level of care, often without the same regulatory restrictions nursing home providers have to meet.

We even see assisted living providers out-sourcing these care services but giving the appearance of providing them internally. Consumers are staying home or going anywhere except into your nursing home beds.

What is good for the consumer is bad for your business and your bottom line.

Political priorities are a driving factor in this too. Let's call it what it is. As the politics of health care continue ramping up, a key factor impacting senior living providers into the future is going to be the continuing shift of political priorities and decisions about where money is spent.

Because many referrals to nursing homes come from hospitals, it is growing more essential for senior living providers to understand what is driving discharge referral patterns. Just as competition and market force pressures are impacting senior living, they are impacting the hospital providers as well. Consider the three major eras in which hospitals have operated since the dawn of the twentieth century.

Charitable Era: (1900 to 1960): In this era, the focus was on providing care to the community, no matter the cost. You were making a difference in your community and so were the hospitals who were your community partners or owners.

Technology Era (1960 to 1990s): This was the period in which major medical transformation was really starting to shift what the hospitals were focusing on, so you started to see MRI equipment and other technology being deployed in all of the hospitals closest to you.

Economic Era (Today): Today it is all about the money. Money is what is driving decision-making. The market force of health care utilization is being driven by the economics of care. These trends are now affecting you on a daily basis. Money is being driven by politics and the political influences of those who lobby. The population needing care, especially the burgeoning number of older adults, is overwhelming the budget available to pay for it. Shifts into managed care and managing the available financial resources are impacting decisions on healthcare delivery and usage.

Perhaps some of you are in states not being as affected yet by managed care or the Accountable Care Organizations (ACOs) that were set up as part of the Affordable Care Act under what is often referred to as Obamacare. The early results of ACO involvement on nursing home providers we have seen in markets in which they were established have been significant.

In most parts of the country where there is an ACO, you are already dealing with the impact. In one large urban area we worked in, our client was trying to deal with the demands and expectations of three different ACO's. Wrap your head around that. Three different enterprises are trying to sort out how they manage population health, trying to figure out how they manage the limited financial resources, and now are also closely scrutinizing discharges to home health, hospice and nursing homes.

One other trend we have also begun to see in the emerging implementation is aggressive pressure to reduce the average length of stay in nursing homes for post-acute and short-term care. Think about it this way: your hospital provider discharges a patient to your post-acute setting or short-term rehabilitation center because their ACO is putting their hospital under pressure to move the patient along to lower cost areas of the continuum. The hospital is too expensive, so they shift the patient to your nursing home. But you also are quite expensive.

In the ACO environment, or in any kind of capitated payment reimbursement system, the goal will be to place patients in the lowest cost setting and minimize the length of time they stay there. They will seek to move the patient through a continuum that maximizes the profit on the episode of care.

The same thing is holding true for those in markets that have a growing acceptance of Medicare Advantage. Again, the money motive appears. This is impacting nursing homes, home health care, and hospices. The key is to make sure you understand the impact on the variables you are using for your revenue assumptions. Then consider the worst-case scenario, as you just might end up experiencing it.

What is happening in markets where this capitated payment approach operates is resulting in a reduction in the average length of stay for post-acute patients. In many markets, you used to be able to rely on a 25- to 30-day stay for each referral. But if your average length of stay drops due to this capitation pressure, you are going to get hit hard financially. We have seen some clients dropping down to 16-day average stays or less, depending on the payer source. This reflects a drop in nearly one-half of the days they used to be able to generate revenue on for each admission. Unfortunately, there are often not enough additional hospital discharges for those admissions to make up for the lost patient days.

So suddenly, nursing home providers are getting slammed because they budgeted with the expectation of a much longer stay for each patient. If there are not enough additional patients being discharged from the hospitals in your market to make up those lost patient days, you could end up in serious financial trouble. I have seen clients struggle with this shift due to the ACO pressure and it is not pretty. It also happened so rapidly they missed it. The real problem is they were so focused on their day-to-day operations, they did not anticipate the challenges or pressures of their hospital referral partners until the impact was dropping to their bottom line.

The other problem with this ACO development is this is not a proven concept for long-term care providers. As hospitals experiment with these new capitated models of payment, the impacts on patient care are still unknown. They may even start shifting the oldest and most frail older adults into hospice, rather than continuing to invest in medical care because the cost to maintain their lives is too expensive. As one hospital planner admitted to me, shifting to hospice is "a more efficient utilization of scare resources." Yes, he actually said this. It has yet to be determined what impact being shifted to hospice has on a patient and their family.

We can only imagine the impact on providers when the demographic Tsunami finally hits the age group we provide care services to. It is not just that there will be a huge number of people who need care, but demographically we won't have enough access to employees to provide quality care. Plus, the government programs of Medicare and Medicaid that the industry relies on to pay for care will very carefully deploy their limited budget resources.

Keep in mind what is happening to you is also happening to other providers. You likely have a lot of competitors who are trying to figure out how they're going to try to deal with the financial pressure as their patient days also drop or their referral sources dry up.

What I am finding in markets dealing with this capitated care management approach is many providers are being blind-sided. When I talk to their teams, most do not understand what is driving the situation. There is little critical thinking. They are looking for simple answers to explain it and often say, "Oh, the hospitals are just discharging more people to home health."

Yet when I buy hospital discharge data to evaluate if this is really true, we often end up proving that it is the reduction in length of stay days that is having the major impact. This industry shift is complicated by government intervention in the payment for care episodes and the evolving implementation of these government theories of how care should be managed is challenging for all providers.

This reduction in the average lengths of stay and the increased competitive pressure is taking even very large and sophisticated providers by surprise. They have been hit over the head with a two-by-four trying to sort out what they are going to do to deal with this.

Unfortunately for some, they have invested millions of dollars in creating state of the art post-acute buildings they can no longer keep full because the hospital partners they initially collaborated with have shifted their post-acute strategy. If the hospital had little skin in the game, often they will not be as mindful of the impact on your finances if they change their plans. We have seen this happen.

The risk of relying on government-compensated services creates a vulnerability which is going to continue to fluctuate from election cycle to election cycle. Who knows what the next election cycle will bring or what new rules will be established impacting payment and care delivery. Whether it is an ACO, Medicare Advantage, or some other evolving capitated payment system as government continues to make changes to health care, the revenues generated from these programs remains exceptionally vulnerable.

Medical Advancements:

Another market force impacting the senior living industry is the significant medical advancements that are taking place. Advances in medical technology are expected to provide the elderly with a lifestyle of greater independence. Advancements in the medical profession have promoted a variety of home health programs and devices. As the variety of home health options increases, this may delay the need for nursing home care for a longer period of time or allow some elderly to avoid this setting altogether.

Advancements in research are finding solutions to medical challenges at an unprecedented pace. This means the elders we now care for are often living with much more complex medical needs and they are living longer. Even ten years ago, many of them would not have lived through their illnesses or conditions.

Older adults are also living more vibrantly than would have been expected in the past. They are living more successfully with chronic conditions. Joint replacements are offering them better ambulation and the potential to continue to live independently. You need to ask yourself how medical advancements and technology will impact the need for your nursing home beds and other services.

I have had recent conversations with senior living industry leaders who privately predict at least 25% of nursing homes existing today will be closed within the next five to ten years. They predict there will be another 25% or so of nursing home providers that will really struggle but will manage to hang on. Another 25% will do well enough that they will have some breathing room and will be able to do some re-investment. Finally, there will be 25% who will do really, really well, and will endure.

What do you do? Think about it from your consumer's point of view. As a resource in your market, you can be a credible source of information about how people age. You observe the aging process every single day. Why not become thought leaders in your market to share your insights?

There are many snake oil salesmen out there right now trying to tell older adults how to live and what vitamins to take to impact their health. There are also some sketchy operators entering this industry intending to make a significant profit who have no idea what they are getting into or how to ensure quality care for the vulnerable adults who have been entrusted to them. Use your experience and wisdom to guide the conversations about the true consequences and outcomes of aging. Help consumers make better choices about the care they seek for themselves or their loved ones.

A senior living competitor in a market I was researching was promoting his determination to cure dementia. He is installing lights around his building to simulate night and day. He is creating little neighborhoods so residents have house fronts at the entry to their apartment. Conceptually, this sounds okay to me; but he is feeding on the fears of the consumer and her family who is terrified of dementia. His sales pitch is all about how he will "diminish _**all**_ the symptoms of dementia." How can he legitimately make this claim? Other senior living providers tell us they have repainted their facilities in calming colors of blues and greens to "soothe" their residents. It might help, but it is a long way from a cure.

As professionals in this industry, you know how impossible this is. Every time you turn around there is someone selling another vitamin to take care of memory loss. You may have heard about research being conducted in another country studying how they are using ultra-sound to break up the plaque in mouse brains. If the evidence ultimately shows this approach works, it would not surprise me to see people coming out in a few years to offer mobile ultra-sound units to wave a wand over people's heads with the promise it will make a difference in brain function or break up the plaque causing Alzheimer's.

The point here is consumers are desperate for answers and the snake oil salesmen will sell them answers whether they work or not. The actual research being done at esteemed medical facilities is much more complex, cautious, and realistic that Alzheimer's and other forms of dementia are far from being easily fixed with paint colors and vitamins.

Renowned geriatricians we have interviewed tell us the current evidence-based medical research shows the best ways to improve cognitive and physical health are to exercise regularly, eat right, socially engage with others, and stay mentally active. How interesting that all of those resources are generally offered in most senior living communities and are offered with the encouragement to get and stay involved.

For those who have already been diagnosed with dementia, sometimes the best therapies are lower tech. One of our clients uses doll therapy with their memory care residents. This therapy of using a lifelike baby doll offers purpose and meaning as the resident becomes a caregiver for the doll. Our client has observed these residents having decreased anxiety, increased social interaction, and improved mood. Other clients incorporate music therapy and aromatherapy into their resident experience to reduce stress and increase connection.

As providers, you play a unique role in helping educate the marketplace on our industry and its benefits. You can leverage the trend of consumers having a deep desire to learn how to age well. You can be the subject matter expert on aging who becomes their trusted ally. Develop and market yourselves as trusted thought leaders on aging in your communities.

Case Study #5

One of the nation's most widely regarded senior living providers was developing a continuing care retirement community in Colorado. The independent living component was already in pre-sale. Previous restrictions imposed by the State of Colorado on the development of nursing home beds had created an urgent need for management to re-evaluate their development sequence and consider if the nursing home and assisted living components of the project should be developed sooner than they had planned.

Interviews with local health care and human services professionals identified market needs for specific levels of care, referral patterns, competition strengths and weaknesses, market expansion plans, as well as critical success factors for the proposed development. A review of historical state nursing home use rates determined significant downward trends and identified serious potential challenges if the development was delayed. A deep dive into the demographic data identified several key target markets to be served and the expected changes in market potential for assisted living and nursing home beds. New opportunities for post-acute and Alzheimer's care services were also identified by the demographic review.

By obtaining and reviewing detailed market information, management was able to make better decisions regarding the staging of the campus development. Today the campus offers a full continuum of care.

Chapter 9
The Strategic Impact of Other Market Forces

Other market forces are also impacting senior living providers to varying degrees. As with any industry in a period of transition, these changes will create new business opportunities for those who understand and capitalize on the emerging market conditions. Those who ignore these market forces or do not take them seriously may wind up in financial distress or go out of business.

Economic Influences:

The stability of our economy is another market force that plays a major impact on our industry. As noted earlier, recessions typically occur in a six to seven-year cycle. While it has not been since the early 1980's that we have had one as dramatic as the Great Recession, some of these recessions have been very difficult for providers and for the residents we hope to serve.

History tells us we will continue to be dealing with an evolving economy. The timing for when another recession will kick in is a critical uncertainty. But it is inevitable that it will happen. Make sure you always anticipate and prepare for the eventuality of a future recession so you are not caught off-guard. Have at least some of your worst-case thinking in play and talk about what you would do. By imagining the potential impact of the complexities and velocity of the change in the world around you, you are less likely to be completely caught by surprise. It is also important to get your team to develop their own critical thinking skills when they are not under intense pressure. You must be prepared to adjust in order to continue to succeed if the uncertain economy becomes traumatic yet again.

It is imperative to your enterprise survival to have a well thought out back up plan for an economic downturn. For example, think about what expenses you can cut temporarily or permanently without impacting your residents' comfort and safety? Are there services you can outsource rather than paying for full-time staff? Can you pull back on some printed or broadcast marketing materials while relying on developing a more robust (and free) social media presence? Have you reviewed administrative salaries with an eye on "spreading the pain" of budget cuts? Have you considered engaging in fund-raising to set up a more robust rainy-day fund? An experienced advisor can help you develop a "What If?" plan that can help ease you through a downturn. Engaging in a brainstorming session with your team can also identify options to consider.

Capital Markets:

Easy access to capital markets are driving some of the excesses in development activity we see today. This is due to the expectation that there is a lot of money to be made given the projected demographic evolution and the ability to obtain lower-interest rate financing. As a result, many new players are entering the industry with limited insight into its many intricacies.

I get calls like this nearly every week, "Hi Jill. I just need you to do a quick study so I can get my financing." They don't want to do the deeper dive to assess the competitive environment or the detailed demographics. They just want a fast and inexpensive study so they can get their financing and move forward with the construction on their development. We find these "quick study" engagements have vastly more financial and operational risks. Our experience shows when clients have relied on these quick studies, they often end up calling us because they turned into distressed properties or communities in need of a turnaround.

It is amazing to consider that investors who are willing to finance millions of dollars in construction and development costs will balk at investing the money to make sure they are developing something that truly matches their market. An in-depth approach to research is valuable and a much better fit with organizations who want to manage the complexities of entering into or expanding their footprint in this industry.

Quick and superficial does not necessarily mean accurate. Comprehensive market research provides you with a much clearer picture of the options, your opportunities, and your potential risks. This is especially true for existing operators who need to deal with the consequences of the new developments coming into their markets.

Novice developers who have not been involved in the senior living industry often do not understand the reality of the complex dynamics of the elder care market. Nor do they understand the target market trends or demographics we have been reviewing in this book. They are just buying real estate and building the framework for these spaces. They assume they can just hire the talent they need to run them.

Newsflash: staffing in senior living is exceptionally difficult right now. Finding the talent you need to operate a business you know nothing about adds a significant business model risk to a novice senior housing developer. Even those of you who understand this business know the enterprise risk is challenging, especially because you are really selling services that rely on the talent and expertise of your team.

With so many investors considering getting into this business, there are many developers looking at how they can encroach on your market. They are adding their new buildings and units because their feasibility study of those ages 75+ "proved" there was a market for them. They might be thinking (or more likely dreaming) that their snazzy new building will attract residents from other, often distant, market areas – unaware of the importance of community ties and nearby family. They are planning to take away your prospects. They are hoping for the best with little understanding of what it really takes to operate successful and enduring senior living communities. Hope is not a strategy that works in any business.

Relatively easy access to money and new competitive development is creating market pressures for many long-standing providers who need to learn how to compete more effectively for their market share. This is going to continue to impact providers as long as there is money available for development and inexperienced developers dreaming of the money they will make from the "Senior Tsunami."

Yet as noted earlier, with the demographic bubble now clustering in the younger 75 to 79 age cohort, we could be as much as a decade away from having enough prospects to generate the financial impact all these investors are hoping for in this sector. But in a decade, will those who have aged to the typical admission age truly be able to afford the costs of the living environment, especially after a decade of compounded annual price increases?

Government Regulations & Reimbursement:

In our industry, government involvement is typically government intrusion, often by people with little knowledge of senior care. Their impact on the industry is another market force that has a significant impact on everything from how you operate, how you staff, what you get paid, and even to the minimum wage you have to pay your team.

I wish the politicians making laws and political appointees setting rules had a deeper level of insight into the complexity of how much they are changing your world. Many of them have no clue – regardless of party – as to the dramatic shifts that are happening or the added burdens they are placing on you that often don't improve the quality of patient care, safety or access.

Do you ever feel like you have whiplash when reading about national health care policies? It's exhausting. And it is not going to end with the next election cycle. Or the one after that. Or the next one. Policymakers don't typically understand (or care) that every time they make a change or cut your reimbursement, there is a trickle-down consequence affecting you and your ability to deliver quality care to those who have been entrusted to you. Those of you offering nursing beds are working with the most vulnerable people we have in our communities. Unfortunately, the reimbursement dynamic is getting more compressed as managed care moves into the Medicare and Medicaid payment arenas.

So much of the time in the senior living industry, we have historically been in a reactive mode. We waited until decisions were made to us, not with us, and then we were stuck trying to figure out what to do to survive. Even now that our industry associations are taking a strong stand and are growing in their ability to influence legislation, there is still much push back from well-meaning legislators who resist listening to this industry insight and experience because they have a different political agenda.

If you start to wrap your head around these complexities early enough, maybe you will not have the perfect answer but you will develop a much deeper insight to anticipate how government changes may affect you in the future. Your survival will require you to anticipate as many of the changes as possible. Your membership in our industry associations will take on significantly greater value as they keep you abreast of emerging changes and help to halt legislation or policy changes that will have a negative consequence.

Your strategic thinking needs to be molded around the What-Ifs. What if they stop talking about it and actually cut rates and resources to the Medicare and Medicaid programs? What if your hospital referral patterns change? What if you cannot get enough team members to staff the beds you have available? You get the idea. What is your most potentially catastrophic What-If?

If you are running a post-acute care unit, you know this all too well. As noted earlier, how are the evolving models for managing reimbursement, such as Accountable Care Organizations, going to impact your average length of stay? It also impacts whether your patient will be covered by Medicare or some other insurance. What will happen if they have to pay out of pocket for their post-acute stay?

Hospital administrators have told me that Medicare auditors are closely examining them. If a patient is admitted as being covered by Medicare, the auditors are quick to scrutinize the admission and may institute a clawback to take back the money that has already been paid for the admission. This can be exceptionally costly to the hospital. When in doubt, the hospitals will put a Medicare patient on Observational Status. While the patient has been in the hospital for three days, their family assumes they will meet the requirement to be covered by Medicare when they are discharged to a post-acute bed in your nursing home.

Consumers have been stunned to find out that Observational Status does not count toward the time required to qualify for Medicare coverage. As a result, the patient may have hospital expenses that are not fully covered and some or all of the costs in your post-acute unit may not be covered either. This single post-acute care episode may eat up $20,000 to $40,000 of what little net worth Mom has if there is no coverage. Then even if she wants to, she won't have enough money to come live in your independent or assisted living apartment. You see the vicious cycle; it's very tough.

By the time you are reading this, who knows what new rules or fixes or regulations the government will have implemented on a state or federal level. But given the budget pressures at all levels of government, it is unlikely that any fix will benefit you to any significant degree over the long-term. And it is a given that something new will be emerging on the local, state or federal level that will continue to impact you in the future.

Technology:

Another market force impacting senior living settings is the on-going array of new technology that may prove to be game changers for the industry. Personal devices and programs may improve resident health status, social interaction or cognition. Robotics may impact staffing and resident interactions. Productivity of staff may be enhanced by use of hand-held technology and remote communication interfaces.

There are many emerging technologies for seniors. There are games and apps for iPads and computers to track health information, remind older adults to take their medications or that can help them learn a foreign language. Computer games like Wii Fit can be used to enhance balance and physical fitness. Apps such as Skype or FaceTime allow older adults to communicate with family members and friends. Sensor technology can be used to monitor the safety of older adults in their homes or apartments. GPS devices and apps can provide instant access to location information and can even gauge a senior's balance and stability as she moves throughout your campus.

I recently saw a photo of a retirement community in Denmark. The fitness instructor was standing on the table leading a class and getting the residents to participate. He was not an instructor in the traditional sense. He was a robot named Zora. It would not surprise me at all if technology becomes incorporated into how we offer companionship in the future. The lack of available staffing may one day mean we have to incorporate robotics into how we offer care. Other countries are already moving into the use of robotics. You might have to one day too.

A few months ago, we studied an assisted living provider who was using virtual reality to engage with residents. Virtual reality was used to connect with these residents in a stimulating way while at the same time allowing staff the ability to provide care to other residents or to work on other matters. Virtual reality may provide opportunities for an independent resident to travel, exercise or even interact with others from far away. The possibilities of this technology are limitless.

You may want to consider how you can use lower tech resources like iPads for service so your nurse can make notes in a resident apartment or room, rather than having to go back and forth to her office to make notes. If she can be more efficient by using technology in her hand, this could increase her efficiency and responsiveness to your residents. Having multiple touch screens on the walls in the hallways of your nursing homes can be used by your nurses and aides. This will save them time and steps. An added benefit is your staff are more visible and readily available to your residents because they are not sitting behind a desk and typing onto a screen.

Think about your Certified Nursing Assistants (CNAs) – they are a major talent pool you need that many industry providers are having trouble finding and keeping. Perhaps there is a way you can use technology to have your front desk receptionist immediately answer when a call light goes off by remotely responding and asking, "Hi Mrs. Jones, how can I help you? What do you need?" before your CNA drops everything they are doing to run to a room to help a resident who just wants a sip of water. You know this happens. If your team members know how urgent the call is or what the resident needs, they can make sure they bring the right resources to the room rather than have to backtrack to get something. Anything that enhances their productivity is good for them, your residents' care, and your bottom line.

Technology has the potential to transform how we provide optimal care. It will be a key not only to efficiency and effectiveness in your operation, but given the growing challenges in finding staff, technology is also likely to provide you with other options to do more with fewer team members.

Technological improvements and workforce development cannot be looked at separately. No matter what kind of living environment you offer, everybody is having the same issues and challenges with finding and retaining a reliable workforce. Many of you are not paying enough to attract and keep workers. You waste time and money on hiring, training, and cycling through workers who leave you. Then you have to do it all over again to replace those who left. That is expensive. It might make more sense to pay them a bit more so you can keep them and gain benefits from their long-term employment with you.

In many markets, there are just not enough available workers because there is so much competition. Everybody is chasing after the same people you want to hire. Five or ten years ago, you would have had more than an adequate supply of potential employees. Today you have hospitals looking for workers. Add to the mix the growing number of senior living competitors, home health care agencies, and other senior focused providers who are all chasing after the same employees you need for your communities. Now add all the new development activity and you have even more providers trying to hire from the same limited talent pool, sometimes offering bonuses for new hire referrals. This pressure for staff is not expected to end soon.

It's time to start thinking outside the box and act like a Millennial who was born with a smartphone in her hand. You have to leverage technology in ways that allow you to deal with some of the challenges you already have and will continue to face in the future. Brainstorm how these emerging technologies can be incorporated into your service delivery to increase the productivity of your team or enhance your resident experiences. Then start budgeting or fund-raising now to begin to take advantage of them.

Affinity Relationships

Some of you are involved with providers who have a resident base that is affiliated with a unique interest group. This can be a religious faith, fraternal organization, college or some other external entity that creates special ties among those who belong to it. Affinity relationships can be an amazing referral source for a provider and those deep ties can provide long-term opportunities to add residents to a site who come from much further away than would be expected for a normal local market geographic boundary.

Your strategic considerations must also ensure that you continue to maintain ties to these key referral sources and affinity organization's gatekeepers of information about your site. You cannot get complacent and assume these relationships will always remain in place. People you had a referral relationship with leave for other opportunities and those who replace them may have existing relationships of their own with other providers. Affinity organizations can change their strategic direction. They also experience changes as their prospect and/or membership market changes. Their membership base can change or they may not be as strong as they were years ago.

If you rely on an affinity or affiliate relationship to provide you with a substantial portion of your residents or referrals, you are highly vulnerable to their on-going success. Typically, you cannot influence what happens with them. You are reliant on them. Pay close attention to the affinity groups you are connected to and be alert to elements impacting their strategic success. Look for data and information that will help clarify their stability so you can understand and anticipate any changes. Understand how their use of emerging communications and social media options may provide you with new options to reach your affinity-connected prospects. Above all, don't take it for granted that they will always be the dominant referral source to your site.

Case Study #6

A 75-year old long-term care provider affiliated with a fraternal organization had historically focused on providing nursing home beds and board and care services. Their 80-acre campus was undergoing a major expansion and renovation so they could begin offering a full continuum of care. The development was not only resizing the mix of current services on the campus, but was adding a number of new service options. These new options included development of a post-acute transitional care unit, dementia unit, assisted living apartments, cluster homes, a clinic, and a town center. The new services and units were all coming on-line at the same time and the organization was experiencing stress because of the turmoil of construction, as well as the anxiety of trying to define the services that were outside their traditional care model.

Staff was inexperienced in marketing and effective promotional efforts because they had historically been able to rely on referrals from the fraternal organization with which they were affiliated to fill their beds. Those affiliate relationships had not been expanded in anticipation of the added unit capacity. A review of the affiliate organization identified it had experienced a decline in membership. It was highly unlikely the provider was going to be able to fill the expansion units from those affinity relationships. This news was a major shock to the leadership team and the board of directors.

Innovative promotional tactics were developed to build a broader base of support for the project expansion from the provider's other referral sources, the local health care community, and to build stronger relationships with the surrounding local neighborhood. An integrated marketing plan was developed to focus resources (staff, time, and money) and coordinate the opening. Strategies were developed to preserve and maintain the appeal to its core affinity-based target market while expanding its local customer base.

The provider achieved accelerated market acceptance of all their new services and attained their business goals well ahead of schedule. They developed a marketing plan to help them recruit more than 70 new employees to service this major expansion. This campus successfully integrated the expansion and is now the home to nearly 450 residents.

Chapter 10
The Strategic Impact of Programming

Programming in your senior living community is an essential element that determines who will be attracted to you and if your target market will be happy once they move into your site. Each area of your customer service must match your prospects and residents in terms of what you offer for activities, fitness and wellness resources, dining options, and how you create a sense of community. Your programming also has to be carefully woven together into a package of services that balance profitability, staff productivity, and that your consumers value.

Scope Creep

Our consumers want more from us today, don't they? They want everything under the sun but they don't want to pay for it, right? Some of you are dealing with scope creep. The term scope creep refers to a subtle process that starts with small adjustments in program offerings and results in services that go far beyond what was originally envisioned or covered by your pricing.

You may be bundling additional services into your care and programming that your residents are demanding. This bundling of services is driving up your costs. It is also impacting how your consumers decide if you are the right fit for them. Younger seniors are not going to be attracted to a highly bundled set of services they do not need or want.

In some cases, your residents are receiving additional services but not paying any extra for them. It often starts with the little things, like having your home health aide who is in an apartment to help the resident with dressing or a medication reminder. Now she takes a few minutes to make a light breakfast for the resident by cooking a scrambled egg or making some toast. Then she straightens up the apartment a little or gets some item down from a closet shelf that the resident cannot reach. It is not uncommon to discover this is happening, but staff may not be telling you because they want to serve your resident. To your staff, this is just an extra service that does not take much time. To you, it impacts their productivity and your profitability. For the resident, they get that extra service they want without having to dip into their cash to pay for it.

Many providers report to us their residents expect additional services they don't want to pay for. The people you hire have a strong desire to provide care and service. This often results in them doing more for residents than they track. Even if you have a good system to bill residents for added services, if your staff doesn't track their time or the care they provide, you cannot bill a resident for it.

Residents are often quite good at cajoling "a little extra help" out of your well-meaning caregivers. They need help with just one little thing. Then another little thing. Those little things can add up to big costs and productivity issues for your team. This results in significant costs to your organization. Those costs can be noteworthy when they are uncompensated due to scope creep.

You must find ways to balance your consumers' wants and needs. You also need to better educate your potential residents about what you offer and what it costs. They need time to plan their budgets and make sure they spend their money in ways that don't deplete all their resources if they expect to live with you.

Activities Programming

Your residents want and need a sense of purpose and a reason to get up in the morning. The days of warehousing elderly residents are over. Don't just bring people in to sing or dance to amuse your residents. It can be entertaining from a performance standpoint, but as an activity, it is like staring at a television where there is no interaction.

Activities and programming are moving beyond working on simple craft activities to while away the time. Residents want to experience the arts. In some communities, the Craft Room needs to be modified to become an Arts Studio. If your beauty shop still has those 30-year old dryer chairs with the big hoods, perhaps it is time for a more modern upgrade. Buy some round brushes and a few hand-held hair dryers. Better yet, spruce it up and convert it into a Spa and Salon and offer some additional services.

Walk around your campus and consider if you need to re-name some or all your common areas. Then consider if there are any needed programming shifts that you might need to make as well.

Challenge your residents to think about different opportunities. Challenge them to be creative and move outside their comfort zone. Bring in educational opportunities to keep their minds sharp or to stimulate them. Your residents are still capable of learning. Your residents are not going to be rocket scientists and program a trip to Mars anymore, but they still care deeply about what's happening in the world. They are still interested in learning. They still remember things from world history and can study current events. Ask them what they want to learn about.

You can use online resources which are popular and cost-effective. Or, you can connect with local people in your community to do it as well. Bring in speakers that encourage your residents to think beyond their own walls. Even incorporating new technologies such as virtual reality glasses can open their worlds beyond the limits of age. The key is to offer a wider array of more vibrant programming.

Consider your use of resident committees or a resident leadership council. Yes, involving them in anything that might influence decision making will likely become the bane of your existence, but their participation can also be another forum for your residents to still feel like they have a say in the world around them. Your residents may have lost control of most aspects of their lives; you can give some back to them. They can also be a wonderful resource to ensure your programming is interesting and engaging.

Look for collaborative partners to work with you on implementation, especially if your budget is tight. You do not have to do this all alone. Nor do you have to spend a fortune to do these things. If you are clever and reach out to people in your local community, you may find they are looking for venues and opportunities for showcasing their programming. Then you can collaborate with these partnerships to benefit your residents. Maybe you can trade the use of your community room if in return someone will do a wine tasting class or teach your residents an art class. Being clever and creative is another way for you to be able to stand above your competition. Don't be afraid to innovate.

Then keep circling back to keep the creative strategies coming and test how well they work. I also encourage you to begin to innovate by first starting with a pilot program. This allows you to test your change in a small and controlled way first so you can work out the kinks before you move it into a bigger project that costs a lot more money.

Fitness and Wellness Programming

The older adults from the GI Generation often sat in their living room and watched the Godfather of Fitness, Jack LaLanne, do his exercises on their televisions. They did not exercise with him, they just watched him do it. Today your residents are expecting you to offer access to elder-friendly exercise equipment, diverse classes, and/or personal trainers to help them maintain their functional fitness.

Who would have ever thought we would have yoga or Tai Chi classes offered in our senior living communities? But it's an important dynamic because this new group of Silent Generation seniors is looking for programming that allows them to remain vital and stay this way as long as possible.

The fitness and wellness aspect of our industry is also evolving because it offers our residents significant health benefits. Exercise gets the synovial fluid in their knees moving. It stretches their hamstrings so they can walk better. Their bones stay stronger and they have better overall balance.

These health benefits can help your residents remain more independent and not have to rely on other services. Exercise classes create opportunities for socialization and build a sense of community. Physical activity also impacts cognitive health. If active seniors are going to ambulate and be physically healthier, they may not need your nursing home beds or they won't need them for as long.

Early in my consulting career, I had a client who had installed a swimming pool. Unfortunately, it was a very expensive amenity because the only people who ever used it were grandchildren who occasionally came in to visit. Now providers are building indoor Olympic-sized pools heated to the perfect temperature to compete for residents who want to be active and social while taking advantage of an exercise resource that is easy on the joints. Or as one resident told me, he wanted to be able "to sit in the hot tub and have a good soak."

Residents today want more from their exercise programs because they want more out of life. Some of them even want to be more challenged in their fitness programming. They are not content with sitting in a chair and throwing a beach ball to each other. They want more challenging fitness programming that will enhance their health and vitality.

Of course, you need to make sure they are safe when they are doing these things. Some providers are now offering tiered fitness programs to accommodate the different fitness levels of their residents. Many are offering these programming resources to their assisted living and nursing home residents too. The stronger your residents are, the less strain on your staff if they can assist even a little in transfers or ambulating.

Brain health also is a huge factor. Former President Ronald Reagan was one of the first to publicly disclose he was afflicted with Alzheimer's Disease. Seniors live with the fear they are going to develop dementia because everyone talks about it now and many celebrities have developed Alzheimer's or some other condition resulting in dementia. Famous people have come out with their struggles from Glen Campbell to Charmain Carr, who was in the movie The Sound of Music. Renowned women's basketball coach Pat Summit died of Alzheimer's Disease in 2016. There are so many others and even more that will eventually be announced.

Talk about dementia is everywhere and the movie Still Alice with Julianne Moore brought the topic to Hollywood. While it can be frightening, there is much current medical research about the different things older adults can do to positively impact their brain health through nutrition, exercise, on-going learning, and implementing lifestyle management strategies. Have you matched your services and resources to provide your residents with these lifestyle components? The better the match, the more valuable you become to them in achieving their goals for living better and enhancing their quality of life.

Dining and Nutrition

We are also learning more about how nutrition affects healthy aging. You can play a role in that as well. Your residents are looking for options. They want healthier food and they are demanding it too. When was the last time you really evaluated your meal program in terms of nutritional benefits to aging? Does it match what your residents now expect? I have been in communities that have not made this adjustment yet.

This evolving senior consumer also wants variety in their settings. You probably already have a main dining room, a private dining area, and some way for your residents to get a takeout meal. But is this enough? Think about how you would feel if you had to sit and eat one to three meals a day in the same place, in the same area, and at the same table with the same people? Okay, that's how we ate with our families when we were young, right? But this isn't the family dinner table of their childhood.

Some of the communities I have been in are creating more of a sense of community than just assigning residents to a specific table. In one small rurally-located independent living community I recently worked with, the residents decided they wanted to experience family-style dining. They pushed all the tables together into one big long table so they could all be together. Of course, there may be challenges to continuing with this approach in the future, but for now, it is working because everyone has a place at the table. We made sure this level of resident camaraderie became a central focus of their marketing messages.

Think about how you create the dining experience for your residents. What is the quality of the food you offer and does it appeal to them? How does your team welcome them when they come to the dining area? How does your team interact with them during the dining experience? What is the level of warm hospitality offered? How do new residents get integrated into the mix? Dining can be a valuable opportunity to make a new resident feel welcomed and a part of your community.

When I work with a client outside my home-base in Minnesota, I don't like staying at a local hotel. I prefer to stay at the site. I eat meals with the residents to observe how your staff interact with them and get a sense of the dining experience. I guarantee you I see things that most of you don't know are being done. Sometimes, it is not negative, but it can be loving interactions and quiet attention to the unique details of what a resident likes and how they like it. It is silently bringing them a cup of black coffee with two sugar packets or a bowl of mixed fruit with only the berries they like the best. Then those interactions are topped off with a warm smile and welcoming greeting.

These kinds of personal touches make all the difference to the resident experience and their satisfaction. We've all heard about this factor for many years but how many of you are actually executing it? There is likely more that you and your team can do. There is opportunity to go beyond the basics without significant added cost.

Dealing with Isolation

Seniors often get isolated in their own homes as they age. Their world narrows, lifelong friends die, they shut down and stop moving. They wait for visitors to come. They are vulnerable to the scam artists who prey on the lonely elderly. They watch the Catholic Channel 24/7 or cable news non-stop because they cannot remember (or bother) to change the channel. They fall asleep in their recliners and stop using their bed. The only ambulation they have is moving from the chair in the den to go to the bathroom. Then they move a few feet into the kitchen where they use their microwave to cook a frozen dinner or heat their sodium-filled soup.

As senior living providers, you offer services and resources in an environment which minimizes isolation. You and your teams are creating a community in which your residents can find new friends, someone to talk with at dinner, and experience enjoyable activities.

What you offer in your communities is the opportunity for socialization and stimulation, both of which have a cognitive health benefit. Your nutrition programming can help manage cardiac health, diabetes, and other medical conditions. You can create opportunities for people to be able to eat their way to maintaining their health.

While each of these factors is important to healthy aging, most of you don't talk about it in a way that matters to your consumer. You talk about the size of the apartments and how many closets they will have or that they have a washer and dryer in their unit. You brag about your movie theater and the popcorn. You describe the various care venues you offer. Yet rarely when we are shopping your sites do we learn about the hospitality, life and lifestyle "Mom" will enjoy when she lives with you.

Building a Sense of Connection

Despite all of the services and resources you offer, at the end of the day, what your residents are really craving is connection. They connect with your team and with each other. If you look at the opportunities you and your team create, you will find new ways to foster this kind of engagement.

I think a lot of providers just hope engagement will happen organically. Yet you can more effectively manage the experience for your residents. You can manage it by how you bring people in and coordinate the welcome experience for your new residents. Do you do everything possible to make their transition easier and less anxiety producing? Think about how YOU would like to be welcomed into a new home you might not have even wanted to move into at first. For many of your new residents, they are overwhelmed with the move, fearful they won't like your community, and are worried about everything from the expense to whether they will be able to navigate your corridors.

Frankly, you need to be more engaged in your residents' environments because many of you have cliques in your communities. These cliques can make it hard for a new resident to feel welcome. Plus, we all know that just like high school, you may have some Mean Girl cliques in your buildings too. These dynamics need to be addressed so your new residents can make healthy connections and build relationships.

Despite working with the senior living industry for all these years, the impact of a lack of connections and isolation didn't hit home for me until I was dealing with the changing health of my mother-in-law. We were all busy living our lives and I was running a growing business. Gen was lonely. She wanted time with us, but we were handling things for her like grocery shopping and errands. Setting up her medications. Taking her to the doctor. Mowing her lawn. Managing her finances. We were doing everything except just keeping her company by listening and talking.

It wasn't until we began comparing notes about what we each were doing for her that we started to understand just how much help Gen really needed. Maintaining her independence at home was growing impossible. Complicating the situation was the advent of several challenging medical issues and the consequences of her increasing cognitive impairment. Gen finally agreed she needed to move to a senior living community and I found her the perfect location.

Before she moved, Gen confessed to me that she was afraid. "How am I going to meet new people? I don't know how to make new friends."

This conversation broke my heart. Gen was a gracious woman who had always been an exceptional hostess that made everyone feel welcome in her home. Yet now she did not feel she even knew how to make friends anymore. She was also afraid she would not be able to learn her way around a new building. It turned out she was right on both accounts.

Gen's cognitive impairment revealed itself to be much worse once we moved her into the new environment. We discovered she'd been compensating significantly in her home and that her closest friend had helped her secretly compensate more than we knew.

Once Gen moved, I spent hours hiding in her new building, trying not to be seen, just so I could make sure she was learning how to navigate in her new environment. If I saw something was not going well for my mother-in-law, I would reach out to the staff and ask them to intervene. What I observed too with growing sadness was that Gen could no longer hide her cognitive impairment. Her anxiety about living in this unfamiliar place was aggravated by her inability to consistently find her apartment, despite its easy location in the center of the building near all of the common areas.

Then the Mean Girls hit. Those Mean Girls were vicious and they no longer had (or chose) to filter their scathing comments as they spoke to Gen. I remember thinking at the time, "Wow, this is worse than anything I ever saw in high school."

You know exactly what I mean.

So in memory of Gen, please consider how you will take action to manage these situations. How will you create safe spaces for your older adults as they navigate their changes in both their health and cognition? It matters.

Fostering a Sense of Purpose

Another consideration is how you and your teams create opportunities for your residents to establish or maintain a sense of purpose in their lives. They need to maintain a sense of self-worth even though their bodies, their minds, and their relationships are all changing.

The best part of what you can offer to your residents is the value-added service of connection. This should be your purpose in running your enterprise and the focus of how you and your teams do your work. Your residents want to be the best at living the life they have left and they depend on you for meaning and healthy engagement. Discover what roles and activities they have been passionate about and then identify the means to keep them thriving in similar efforts.

My dear friend Joan Kennedy was 92 when we had a party to celebrate her achieving Amazon best-seller status with a book she had written. When she was 94, Joan and I had a lovely dinner at the private club I belong to because she had always wanted to go there. She took an Uber to get there.

As we talked over dinner, Joan revealed, "I have got my goals for the next four months set up." She had plans to write another book and was intending to give speeches on her book topic.

I told her, "Joan, this is why you are doing as well as you are doing at your age. This is also why you are still so cognitively healthy and are moving as well as you move. This is why you are still so present."

Now age 96, Joan recently completed a workbook to serve as a companion to another book she has written. Each day, she focuses on finding meaning and a way to contribute. Of course, genetics and earlier lifestyle choices play roles in how we age. Yet it is having purpose, goals and plans that serve as an "insurance policy."

Think about the opportunities you can create for the Joans in your buildings. You might want to offer some creative writing classes or other activities you have not tried before. Make sure you challenge your team to try offering a few new activities programs because I know some of you are still offering the same old, same old, same old programs. They are boring and stale. Bingo? In today's world? Really? I know you can do better. Yes, I recognize that you have residents who enjoy bingo and you will need to keep offering it. But you need to offer more.

When you think about this generation of seniors, in this phase of their lives they want to know they still matter. Whether your residents are knitting hats for the children who are in the hospital, or sewing gifts for veterans, or helping to build walking paths for the community or gardening fresh produce to donate to a local food shelf, there are things your residents can still do. You can be a conduit for them to make those connections.

Maybe some of the workforce challenges other local employers in your town are having could also provide an opportunity to augment the cash flow for some of your residents. It's a way to get them out into the community. A business owner I know in the gardening and nursery industry said some of her best retail employees are over the age of 65.

Work for seniors does not have to be full-time work requiring a 2,000 hour a year commitment. Part-time work allowing them to be engaged in the workforce could be something mutually beneficial to them and the local employers in your community.

Chapter 11
The Need for Deeper Strategic Thinking

Study after study has been done over the years to identify the skills needed in the workforce for effectiveness and business survival. Typically, those skills include complex problem solving, critical thinking, judgment, and decision-making. Unfortunately, you probably do not have people on your teams who have well-developed expertise with these skill sets. Your teams are so pressured on a day-to-day basis to do the work they need to complete, all they can think about is the latest problem right in front of them. Who has the time to contemplate all the possible impact of these market forces or the potential changes they may need to make in the future? They are focused on getting through today.

The difficult truth is, the senior living industry has invested very little effort in building these skills in our teams. Everything is operationally focused and about dealing with the most immediate crisis or dealing with a complaining resident or family member. There is little energy available to invest in reflective pondering about the bigger strategic impact.

A while back I was talking about this lack of strategic thinking skills with an executive vice president from a very large multi-site senior living enterprise. His observations really clarified this issue for me.

"About 20 years ago, we cut out the assistant administrators in our senior living communities to save a buck," he explained. "Unfortunately, this was the role where many of the future leaders of our communities used to get their training and gain strategic insight. Now we are paying a price for not developing them."

Your teams have little time to step back to look at all the market forces impacting your enterprises. They no longer have the luxury of thinking ahead to consider, "What can we do strategically? Where can we defend against a new competitor coming into our market? Where can we correct challenges that may emerge in the next year? Where are we really going to be in trouble if regulations change?"

Honestly, I am often disappointed by the lack of strategic thought I am running into with client team members when I am working on a turnaround. They are well-meaning professionals who provide exceptional care. Unfortunately, the questions they ask are basic and often not even in sync with the critical issues. Worse yet, they are missing critical insights that should be shared with senior management and your boards so appropriate strategic adjustments can be made long before the crisis can impact enterprise survival. They have never learned how or been asked to think critically about these issues or to ask deeper questions.

Recently I worked with a client on an extinction level situation involving one of their sites. As I was listening to their team members explain to me what they believed the underlying reasons for the problems were, I understood fully how the board and C-level leaders got surprised by what had happened. Nothing those team members told me checked out when we pulled objective data to assess if what they were saying was true. They clearly did not understand the true problems or the underlying fundamentals of what was occurring that had caused the crisis. You cannot solve a problem you do not understand.

By using verifiable data and information, we cracked the code. We uncovered the true drivers of the business issues causing their occupancy problems. We then shared perspective and a clearer overall picture with the senior leaders in the organization to enable them to address the real issues. This became an opportunity to provide those team members with a deeper insight into the critical market forces driving their business. Through this process, they should be better prepared in the future to identify the impact long before it nearly puts the enterprise out of business again.

Ask better questions of your teams. Expect more information and deeper insight from them. Obtain it for them if they don't know how to access it. If they lack true strategic insight, and things aren't going well, you will not be able to rapidly impact the situation before it is completely out of control. If you can't affect the situation, there is no way you will be able to manage or prevent the need for a turnaround.

Years ago, I was involved with a turnaround involving a faith-based community in southern Florida. The on-site staff provided me with their explanation for why they believed they were not full. They reported they could never fill because as a devoutly Christian not-for-profit, they could not appeal to those of a different faith who they perceived dominated the older adult population in their local market. This explanation bubbled up all the way to the C-Suite in the corporate home office. Now those executives believed nothing could be done because they thought the local market forces were out of their control and they had no ability to impact the outcome.

While there was clearly a significant population of older adults of the other faith in the market, and my client was an evangelical faith-based provider, something about this explanation did not ring true. It was too simplistic and no one could show me any data to support this claim. We did some significant side research to determine if what they believed about the faith-based community was really the case. It was not.

It took some digging well beyond a cursory review of the demographic data. After obtaining detailed estimates of those of this faith from a study recently performed by the local religious community and comparing these data estimates to the demographics of the market, it was clear this simple explanation was wrong. Those of this faith group only represented a small, but important, sliver of the older adult population in the area. Demographics based on faith in this situation were not the issue.

The truth of why my client was not full had little to do with the religious dynamics of the local market. It fundamentally had to do with their pricing strategy and a mismatch between the elements of the services they were selling in their contract that did not make sense to the local market. The client was offering a very unique service contract and their competitors were marketing aggressively against them. Prospective residents did not understand the value of the client's contract and instead they went to competitors who were selling a service package that made more sense to them. Further, my client's programming and activities offerings for residents was overly faith-based and this significantly limited their appeal to those of any other religious denominations.

Finally, I asked the client leadership, "How on Earth did this become the explanation for why you are not full?" If people really believe a myth is something they cannot change (such as the number of people of a specific religious faith), then they can give up because they do not think they have any influence in making a difference.

It turns out the myth had been perpetuated by a novice marketing director for the site who had only been there a few months. Her educational background was in the arts and she had very little real-world experience, much less involvement in our industry.

In her inexperienced view, this explanation was the simplest way she could wrap her head around the complex issues impacting her inability to sell units or generate increased occupancy. No one with more expertise ever thought to test her myth. This theory never got challenged and her explanation went up the whole corporate chain. Then everyone began to make excuses for the site's non-performance by viewing it as being out of their control.

For a year and a half, everybody in the organization was operating off of the mistaken assumption they could do nothing. But this explanation had nothing to do with what was really going on in the market and they most definitely had options to resolve the site's occupancy issues. Once the real issues were understood, corrective actions were taken, and the turnaround was successfully completed.

If you are not sure you are getting the right insight from your teams, it is time to ask them some harder questions. Use their answers to then challenge your team further to make sure you move them past any unfounded assumptions. If you ask really good questions, they might not have any answers for you. Keep asking questions. You are going to make people uncomfortable. But you will be better in your job as a leader or board member and they ultimately will be better in theirs – but only if you push and get answers to the tough questions you ask that are based on facts and data, not solely on opinion or hunches.

For those of you who want to begin building the critical thinking of your teams, you can start by asking them questions on a regular basis and testing their answers. Better yet, start by asking a critical question at your weekly staff meeting to get them talking about bigger issues than the latest operational challenge. This approach will begin to hone their ability to ask questions and help each other think more deeply and cross-functionally. Sharing more impactful data and information with them will shake them up, give them some ownership and help them better understand where the vulnerabilities are in your enterprise. There are tools and resources available to provide you with examples of questions you can ask. The key is to ask them.

You need your team members to help you move forward and innovate. You can start to harness their collective insight and intellectual horsepower if you can get them to be more involved in considering the critical market forces shaping your future.

Some of you reading this book offer environments in which your residents move into an independent living setting where the expectation is they will age in place as they require more support and care. Your goal may be to keep them in their current apartment and then use your home health care services. This is revenue after all and you want to keep them living in your community. You don't want them to have to move out to live at one of your competitors in order to access services.

Yet I bet very few of you are doing anything active to create pathways for your residents to get to know your home care nurses or aides, other than at the time when staff finally determines they need to buy the more expensive services. Think about how hard a decision it was for your consumer to move into your site the first time. It is often also a very difficult transition for them to now admit they need to add support services. They are going to worry about the extra costs. Many of them, or their families, are in denial and don't believe they really need any extra services. Adding additional care may also be easy to dismiss because your residents are not comfortable enough with your care team to ask questions or reveal the truth about where they are struggling in their day-to-day lives.

Develop an internal marketing plan to actively promote your home care team and their services. Consider how you develop this internal marketing dynamic to bring your health care talent in front of, and occasionally on the periphery, of your independent residents. You need to engage in opportunities for them to become a trusted adviser who is giving and sharing information with your residents on how to age in place effectively in your building long before they ever need it.

Case Study # 7

The owners of a Michigan-based existing assisted living facility were in pre-sales to add independent living units on its campus to eventually create a full continuum of care. Initial pre-sales of the new units had used a significantly lower price structure than what was now being presented to the market. Resistance to the new prices was strong and only two units had been sold since the price increase had been announced. Management needed to determine why pre-sales were stalled and they also needed a study to submit to the State to obtain technical approval for the independent living development to allow the project to move forward.

Despite having a positive reputation, the market research determined the local community still viewed the campus as being "assisted living." This was due in part to a blurred understanding in the community of what independent living actually meant because other area independent living facilities were functioning more like assisted living. It was discovered that campus marketing staff had not been effective in communicating with prospects about the lifestyle and amenities that would be enjoyed in the independent living component of their campus or in how it would differ from what the market expected.

After a review of the various promotional options used by marketing staff, it was determined that the budget should be redeployed away from investing in local television advertising to other targeted promotional tactics that had a better ability to generate qualified leads. The competitive review also uncovered significant challenges created by the campus' bundled pricing option in comparison to what successful local providers were selling. It was determined that the units be developed in a two-phase process to minimize the market risk for the project.

The State of Michigan approved the project and the new independent living units were constructed. An effective promotional effort focusing on independent living was successfully implemented and a more competitive pricing structure was developed. Once each of these major elements were completed, the site filled and today is a well-regarded senior living community.

Chapter 12
Final Thoughts

Invest the time to focus on understanding how the market forces will potentially re-shape your future as they continue to evolve. Look closely at and think deeply about how each of the market forces is affecting you today. Make sure you get good data and information. Consider how the demographic shifts in your market create potential implications and future opportunities for your organization. Take advantage of trusted advisors who can help you evaluate demographic and other market trends.

This insight will provide you with the best opportunity to anticipate challenges and address them long before they jeopardize your enterprise. This will allow your site leadership, mid-level teams, and your board of directors to stay focused on continually re-calibrating your offerings to ensure you meet the emerging shifts in your market. You can then more effectively assess if what you are doing is going to continue to work. If you do this routinely, you will keep your community moving forward in positive and pro-active ways.

Markets often change around you. It's not you. It's what happens in the evolving community. Your close calibration to the marketplace is critical, especially if you are a long-standing senior living provider. This calibration requires close scrutiny of the demographics, real estate conditions, and all the other factors that come into play. Evaluate how your competitive marketplace is shaping or re-shaping the expectations of your prospects. Continually evaluate the market forces impacting the economy and capital markets. Consider how shifts and changes in healthcare and emerging technological trends can be incorporated into your communities. This includes considering the availability of the caliber of staff you can hire too.

Always ask yourself: "What's the strategic insight we can gain now to change or improve what we do and how we deliver our services or care?" Look at the shifts and changing trends in your market and ask yourself: "How can we innovate in ways we have not ever considered before?"

You hire your executive team for their operational expertise and their caring compassion for older adults. Studying and reading complex markets and the shifts due to evolving market forces is a completely different skill. And it is not a skill you necessarily need on your full-time staff, but it is essential to building strategic depth in your leadership team. Ensuring they have a deeper insight about the intricacies of your local market and the potential consequences of the market forces will provide you with the greater likelihood that they can appropriately respond to emerging shifts long before your site teeters into a compromised situation.

There are no shortcuts. The deep dive takes time and money. But it can make all the difference between long-term survival or bankruptcy. Even if you are currently a strong operator and have a dominant market position, don't assume this will always be the case. Invest in the resources needed to stay on top of your game and your evolving market.

What is needed going forward is a better understanding by boards and executive leadership of the multifaceted variables of the major market forces at play that determine your potential for achieving long-term success. We have seen well-meaning board members attempt to dictate operational or marketing considerations because they did not understand the intricate nuances of this complex industry. Your board education should focus on enhancing their understanding of the multi-faceted market forces influencing your opportunities and potential for survival. This will enhance their ability to be leaders who challenge you and strong partners with you in moving your communities forward to meet the needs of your residents in a fiscally responsible manner.

While I do not claim to have a crystal ball, I do believe our industry is likely going to go through some tough times in the foreseeable future. There will be continued pressure on your occupancy as new providers come online and are absorbed into the market. There will be continued downward pressure on your average length of stay in all levels of your enterprise. There will be continued pressure on reimbursement rates for your nursing home beds and post-acute transitional care services. This is also going to be combined with the growing pressure to maintain or improve your quality ratings, especially if they end up tied to your ability to receive reimbursement.

But remember, you can control how you anticipate your responses. You can look for emerging opportunities. You can work with your team to anticipate needed amenities or other desired resources. You can work with your board to identify fundraising opportunities.

You often have to do more, provide higher-quality care, and offer it for less than you should be paid for in a perfect world. You must figure out where you are making your money and link your thinking about profitability to your strategy. Take this information and align it with your strategic perspective of the market forces. Challenge your teams to have conversations that provide you with insight and understanding so you can fine-tune your strategies or proactively anticipate emerging challenges.

Remember we operate in a VUCA world requiring boldness and innovation to respond to the volatile, uncertain, complex and ambiguous circumstances impacting this industry. Start breaking your critical issues down and discuss them with your team and advisors on a routine basis. Question your assumptions so you can be more strategically flexible.

Try to have fun with what you do even when it's hard. Then link your thinking to the market. Where are the emerging opportunities? It is adding new services or in offering the truly independent lifestyle found in active adult housing? What strategically blends with your market and your experience level within the industry?

At the end of the day though, this is all about what your customers want or need and what they're willing and able to pay for. The difficulty comes when the meaning of willing and able is different than what we think they want, need or are willing and able to pay for. Your challenge is to engage your customers in designing the right package for them – and their pocketbooks.

Ultimately, you have to assess the market risk you are exposed to. All too frequently, senior living providers only look at the overall demographics or consider the potential impact of the initial market forces when they completed their original feasibility study.

Given the velocity of change and the volatile nature of the business and economic climate, you need current market insight. You also need a well-developed ability to translate that insight into a forward view with the consideration of how all these market forces may impact your strategies, team and operational capability.

Too many communities that are at least 20 years old have never had an updated market study done to see if they are still feasible. Then they wonder why they are struggling. Their local market has changed so much with new competition and shifting demographic dynamics that differ from what they were when they originally opened. Often many of these providers are no longer close to being viable due to limited demographics or pricing shifts which created a significant Affordability Gap. Gaining updated market insight is essential for existing providers.

No matter whether you are struggling or are totally full, when I talk to clients about the need to do an updated market study for an existing site on an on-going basis, they often ask, "Jill, do we really need to do this?"

I always answer, "Yes."

I answer this way because I truly believe this is essential. Markets are changing so much, even in rural areas. Getting into the routine of having a comprehensive strategic market analysis done for your site at least every five years will provide you with the objective insight you need to make better decisions and stay attuned to your market.

The important thing to keep in mind is your future is going to continue to change because your customer base is changing. They may have fewer financial resources than we would like them to have and yet they want you to deliver every service under the sun. They want you to do this for free or at very little cost.

Their family members may want this also, but they might have a different motivation for avoiding or begrudgingly paying your bill. The sad truth is some family members do not want to spend money on the care of their elder loved ones because it will diminish their own future inheritance.

Always keep in mind you are working with residents who are going through huge transitions. Even those who are choosing to live in your communities because they want to live with you are still making a big transition. Others are being forced to give up their independence or might be feeling they were pressured into the move by their children. They are losing their physical health and, in some cases, their minds. They are in that uncomfortable part of a major life transition and they don't always know or understand how your senior living community fits into their future. They may view moving into your site as another loss and a huge, irreversible step toward the grave.

The better you can clarify your brand, the better you can clarify what it is you do and offer, the better you will be at helping your residents move into the new beginning of the life they are going to live with you. Think about how you would want your loved ones to be treated when they make what is probably their final move.

Despite all the challenges, what you and your teams do each and every day is significant and difficult. During your toughest days, remember the services you provide to our most vulnerable neighbors and loved ones are important. Take the insight you get from understanding the market forces impacting our industry and bring it down to the individual care you provide. What you do matters to your residents, their families, and to your local community.

Thank you for bringing the best of yourself to a profession that truly makes a difference!

About Jill

Jill Johnson is the President and Founder of Johnson Consulting Services, a management consulting firm based in Minneapolis, Minnesota. Jill helps clients make critical business decisions and develop market-based strategic plans for turnarounds or growth. Her consulting work has influenced more than $4 billion worth of business decisions. She has a proven track record of accomplishment dealing with complex business issues and getting results. Her clients are located throughout the United States, as well as in Europe and Asia. She has won numerous honors for her business acumen, her leadership savvy, mentorship skills, and her entrepreneurial successes. She has also been inducted into two business halls of fame.

Jill has worked with senior living providers throughout the nation to assess their futures in light of the significant changes occurring within the industry. Her work frequently includes evaluation of complex marketplace dynamics and assisting organizations in assessing the impact of these market forces on their long-range strategic plans, master planning efforts, and new service development. Her consulting work to the industry has encompassed the entire continuum of senior living services including active adult housing, independent housing with services, assisted living, memory care, skilled nursing, post-acute care, home healthcare and hospice services.

Jill has been a consultant for numerous senior living clients including two of the nation's Top 10 largest not-for-profit multi-site senior living organizations. She has earned Professional Member status in the National Speakers Association and has the rare ability to deliver substantive content in a way that is engaging and easily accessible. Jill is a frequent speaker for LeadingAge state chapters and other health care industry associations.

Jill has written many published articles on strategy development for retirement housing. Her articles on strategy and marketing issues have appeared in more than 120 magazines. For more than a decade, Jill served as an ambulatory care marketing instructor for the prestigious master's level Health Care Administration program at the University of Minnesota's Carlson School of Management.

Prior to founding Johnson Consulting Services, Jill worked in the national health care practice group in the management consulting division of a major CPA firms which at that time was also one of the largest consulting firms in the world. At this firm, Jill helped develop the methodology for conducting the nation's first assisted living feasibility studies. She conducted the nationwide trend study and wrote the article on it that was featured in the firm's premier national senior living industry publication. She also previously worked for an international management consulting firm.

Jill earned a Bachelor's degree in Business Administration with a double major in marketing and human resource management, as well as a Master's degree in Business Administration from Drake University.

Talk to Jill about how her Consulting Services can help you gain the clarity you need to better understand how market forces are impacting your business strategies. Book Jill to Speak at your next board meeting or staff development event. Contact her at:

Phone: 763-571-3101
Email: Info@jcs-usa.com
Website: www.jcs-usa.com

Acknowledgments

Thank you to everyone who encouraged me to share my professional insight about navigating the complexities of the senior living industry. You made this book possible.

To my clients:

To the many senior living clients I have been honored to work with over the last three decades. Your trust and willingness to go deeper into understanding the market forces impacting your sites has challenged me to be a better consultant and advisor. Thank you for telling me how much this insight about market forces has meant to you and your teams. And thank you for encouraging me to share this insight with others.

To my book team:

Jan McDaniel for helping me pull together my ideas as I pieced together this book. You not only helped me put my words to paper, but also challenged me to write a book that will make those who read it think more deeply about the future of the industry.

Chris Mendoza for your patience in working through the cover design and formatting the content to turn my idea into a reality.

Ann Aubitz for assisting me in getting the printed version of the book to the marketplace.

Joan Kennedy for inspiring me to write and for providing me with deeper insight about aging with vitality and grace.

To my valued insight team:

To the colleagues and clients who took time out of their busy days to review the various drafts of this book and provide me with valuable feedback to narrow the focus down to the most critical information. Your responses and comments have enhanced this content so much! Thank you Mark "Tony" Enquist, Ellen Hoye, Elizabeth Meyer, William S. Myers, Ric Olson, and Aimalicia Staub.

Also Available in the BOLD Questions Series...

Business Strategy Edition

52 questions to shape your
business strategies.

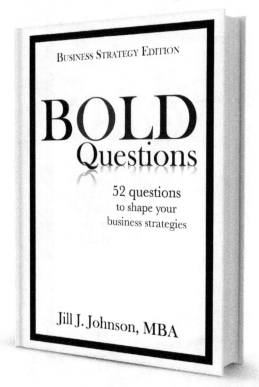

BUSINESS STRATEGY EDITION

BOLD
Questions

52 questions
to shape your
business strategies

Jill J. Johnson, MBA

PURCHASE Your Copy NOW!
Bulk discounts available.

www.jcs-usa.com

Johnson
Consulting
Services
Marketing & Management Consultants

Also Available in the BOLD Questions Series...

Opportunities Edition

52 questions to shape how you
take advantage of your **opportunities.**

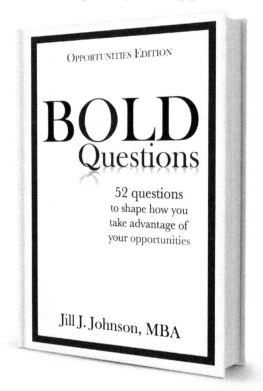

PURCHASE Your Copy NOW!
Bulk discounts available.

www.jcs-usa.com

Also Available in the BOLD Questions Series...

Leadership Edition

52 questions to shape
your leadership **thinking.**

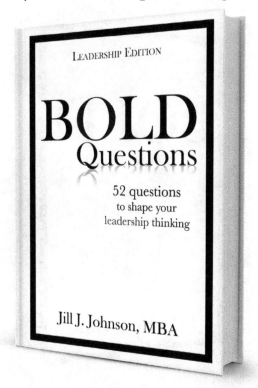

PURCHASE Your Copy NOW!
Bulk discounts available.

www.jcs-usa.com

Also Available in the BOLD Questions Series...

Decision-Making Edition

52 questions to shape
how you make **decisions.**

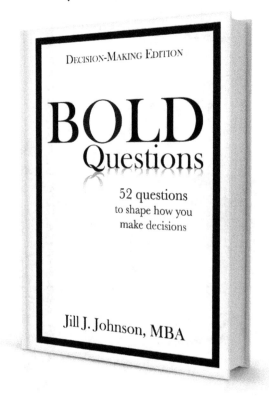

PURCHASE Your Copy NOW!
Bulk discounts available.

www.jcs-usa.com

Also Available...

Compounding Your Confidence

Confidence is one of the most essential skills leaders need to develop and sustain. *Compounding Your Confidence* is a concise blueprint for confidence building and a must-read for anyone who wants to succeed. Packed with humor, stories and wisdom, readers call this international award-winning bestseller "a mentor in a book."

Available on Amazon in paperback, ebook and audiobook formats.

PURCHASE Your Copy NOW!
Bulk discounts available.

www.jcs-usa.com

Johnson
Consulting
Services
Marketing & Management Consultants

Also Available...

Confidence Workbook

Use the *Compounding Your Confidence Workbook* as a blueprint to develop your Confidence Plan to build your confidence as you grow as a leader. Based off the international award-winning bestseller that readers call "a mentor in a book."

PURCHASE Your Copy NOW!
Bulk discounts available.

www.jcs-usa.com

Johnson
Consulting
Services
Marketing & Management Consultants

Also Available...

Recorded Live

Listen to this live recording, of Jill Johnson's
dynamic keynote presentation. You will be transported
into the audience with the 400 other attendees
to learn, laugh and be inspired!

PURCHASE Your Copy NOW!
Bulk discounts available.

www.jcs-usa.com

Johnson
Consulting
Services
Marketing & Management Consultants

CPSIA information can be obtained
at www.ICGtesting.com
Printed in the USA
LVHW010349030320
648723LV00003B/622

9 780998 423654